Cycling Michigan

The 30 Best Road Routes In Western Michigan

By Karen Gentry

PEGG LEGG
PUBLICATIONS

Cycling Michigan
The Best 30 Road Routes in Western Michigan
Published by Thunder Bay Press
Production by Pegg Legg Publications

© 2000 by Karen Gentry
First Edition 1993
Second Edition 2000

Maps by Michele Miller and Pegg Legg Publications
Cover photo and inside Photography by Karen Gentry and Pegg Legg Publications.

Printed in the United State of America

04 03 02 01 00   7 6 5 4 3

ISBN 1-882376-74-9

All information in this book is accurate to the best of the author's knowledge at press time, but is subject to change at any time. Author and publisher assume no liability for inaccuracies.

P.O. Box 580
Holt, Michigan 488842   USA

To those who love to
wander outdoors in Michigan
and all who "eat to ride, ride to eat."
k.g.

30 Bicycle Tours
In Western Michigan

1. Lake Michigan Trail
2. Grand Mere Dunes
3. Sister Lakes
4. Blossomland
5. Amish Tour
6. Kal-Haven Trail
7. Battle Creek
8. Saugatuck Tour
9. Dutch Delight
10. Kent Trails
11. Musketawa Trail
12. Apple Country
13. Fallasburg Fun
14. Squires Street
15. Blockhouse Hill
16. Silver Lake Amble
17. Hart-Montague Trail
18. White Pine Trail
19. Nordhouse Dunes
20. Lake Cadillac Loop
21. Crystal Lake
22. Sleeping Bear Tour
23. Lake Leelanau
24. Suttons Bay
25. TART
26. Old Mission Tour
27. Beethoven Amble
28. Trip Around Torch
29. Hemingway Tour
30. Tunnel of Trees

Contents

Introduction

30 Bicycle Tours

Southwest Michigan

Central West Michigan

Northwest Michigan

Acknowledgments

I've always liked the exhilaration of exercising outdoors. I used to jog outdoors for exercise and fitness but several years ago, a couple of friends of mine convinced me to buy a new bicycle and then invited me on cycling trips. (Thanks, Joan and Gordon!) Since then I've thoroughly enjoyed the camaraderie and the fun of cycling, whether in a large group, with a few friends, or by myself. It's always a grand adventure getting to know people through cycling, discovering new roads or paths, locating a new place to eat or shop and learning the backroads of our West Michigan region.

The idea for this book originated when my friend Joan, an unabashed cycling enthusiast, designed a route in my hometown of St. Joseph/Benton Harbor. We cycled that route a couple of times, in spring and fall, and decided to write an article about it. Later when I was given the opportunity to write a book on bike routes in West Michigan, I was amazed at the excitement and interest that the idea generated. I am deeply grateful to the many friends and family members who supported me on this project.

First of all, I would like to thank all those who cycled with me, helped me map out the routes or offered moral support including Joan, Gordon, Steph, Ann, Tim, Bill, Mary, Jean, Bernice, Cindy, Glennda, Chris and Julie. I appreciate the help from Diane Ruggles from St. Joseph County and June Thaden and other members of the Cherry Capital Cycling Club. A special thanks to Tony for his help with the Sister Lakes and Torch Lake routes. An award should go to Kathy for putting up with me for a week in northwest Michigan. She helped immensely with her knowledge, good-natured humor and ability to read maps, not to mention her enthusiasm for travel and the outdoors. I am grateful to my parents for their love and encouragement. Thanks to my dad for the use of his computer - a real lifesaver - and to my sister, Jane for her computer assistance. I would also like to thank all the people I met along the way and the help from many visitors bureaus throughout West Michigan.

Lastly, I want to thank Libby Richart, who wholeheartedly jumped in on this project. She became a little sick of reading about "tunnels of trees", but she stuck with it. I appreciate her creative talents and all the time and hard work she put into editing this book.

k.q.

Safety And Responsibility

Safety is an important concern in all outdoor activities. No guidebook can alert you to every hazard or anticipate the cycling ability of every reader. Therefore, the descriptions of roads and routes in this book are not representations that a particular excursion or tour will be safe for your party. When you follow any route described in this book, you assume responsibility for your own safety. Under normal conditions, such tours require the usual attention to traffic, road and trail conditions, weather, the endurance level of your party, and other factors.

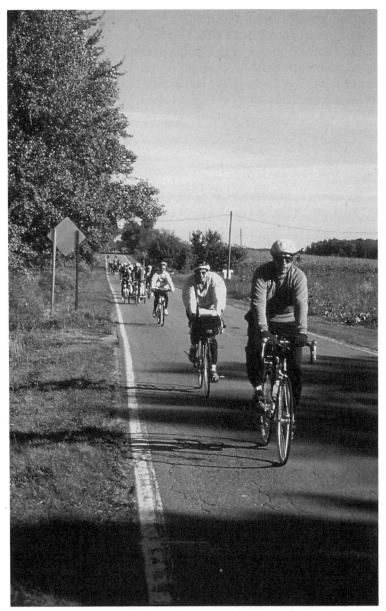

Cyclists participate in the Apple Cider Century ride.

Why West Michigan?

Besides being just darn good exercise, there are three reasons why I cycle. Food probably tops the list. In my cycling crowd, what food to pack and where to stop to enjoy it is an ever popular topic of conversation. Nothing better justifies chowing down than first biking 10, 30 or even 50 miles.

But the second reason occurred to me one afternoon in late September when I was cycling in northwest Michigan, enjoying the crisp air and the warm sunshine. Riding along at a good pace, I slowed down to admire the river up ahead where the trees had just started to change colors, forcing me to take a break.

I pulled over on the bridge and watched the flowing river, felt the gentle breezes and reflected how thankful I was for days like these. As I gazed on the water, I was struck by the beauty and simplicity of the scene. Because of this spot and numerous others in West Michigan, I know why people love to bicycle in this special region.

It could be a gurgling trout stream, a shimmering inland lake, or windswept dunes along Lake Michigan. It could be wildflowers interspersed between rocks, a dense section of hardwood trees, or the smell of apple blossoms. It might be careening down a hill with a panoramic valley and farmland off into the distance or the delight of cycling on a straight, flat, new asphalt bike path. These are the moments that make cycling so special. Although I'm a little partial, West Michigan can give you more moments like these than any other region in the state and maybe even in the Midwest.

The third reason can be summed up by my eight-year-old nephew.

"I want to go with you. My feet might hurt, but I don't care." said Patrick, when he heard about a bike trip I was planning with his parents. A 20-mile loop with hills, cycling over a highway...nah, he's not ready yet. Maybe a stretch of the flat Hart-Montague Trail, perhaps the route around Lake Cadillac - he could handle that.

Patrick's reaction to this particular outing was just another enthusiastic response I received from many people when they found out I was writing this book. All kinds of people of all ages are cycling enthusiasts. Cycling is a recreational sport that fills the urge to be outdoors and to be active, to travel and to explore. Excitement and support from family and friends is definitely what kept me going and kept me inspired to explore the best routes in Western Michigan while writing this book.

Good eating, great scenery and enthusiastic friends to share it all with. What could possibly be better than that?

Why West Michigan?

For this book, West Michigan is defined as the western half of the Lower Peninsula, from Berrien, Cass and St. Joseph counties along the Indiana border to Emmet County on the Straits of Mackinac, to the eastern shore of Lake Michigan (sometimes confusing for you Chicagoans!). The 30 routes in this book range from the southwest corner of the state by New Buffalo to Cross Village in northwest Michigan and include inland areas such as Kalamazoo, Grand Rapids and Cadillac.

West Michigan is blessed with a 1,000 miles of Lake Michigan shoreline, the world's greatest collection of freshwater dunes, hundreds of inland lakes, rivers and streams and endless acres of forests. This scenic, natural beauty is complemented by delightful towns and attractions as well as friendly folks intent on making your stay here a pleasant one.

West Michigan's history is steeped in stories of Indians, French explorers, a lumbering era and a rich agricultural tradition. Many towns are named after our first residents, the Indians; Kalamazoo, Paw Paw, Manistee and Muskegon are but a few. Many West Michigan communities then prospered in the lumbering era. After the Civil War, Michigan emerged as one of the leading lumber-producing regions in the country. The first sawmill in West Michigan

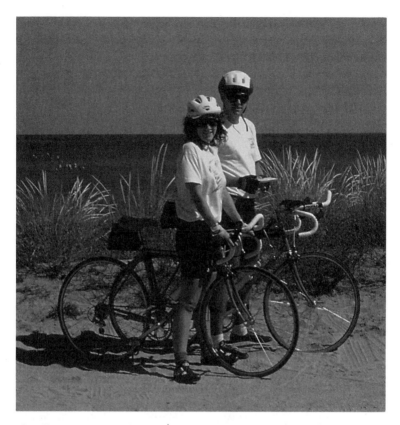

Cyclists pause along Lake Michigan while riding in Old Mission Peninsula in Grand Traverse County.

was built in 1836 in Grand Rapids, followed by another in Muskegon in 1860. Soon mills were built at the mouths of most rivers emptying into Lake Michigan.

Later, the emphasis shifted from rivers to railroads to a system of highways and roadways with the emergence of the automobile. That led to the region's long history of tourism and its eventual name, "Michigan's Gold Coast." The dunes, the beautiful beaches and those golden sunsets melting into the endless blue of Lake Michigan charmed visitors from the days when steamships and ferry boats were crossing over Lake Michigan from Chicago and

Milwaukee. Today, they arrive by car, with their bicycles strapped on top, but they are still looking for many of the same attractions: dunes, beautiful beaches and glorious sunsets.

By cycling the routes in this book, the history of the region comes alive through rail trails, museums, Centennial farms, lumber baron mansions, covered bridges and century-old summer homes. Cycling is an excellent way to find hidden corners and to learn about Michigan's colorful past.

The Routes

This book describes 30 routes, ranging from 4 to 55 miles. It is geared for cyclists of all abilities, with an emphasis on day excursions and cycle touring. Routes can easily be lengthened or combined for a weekend of cycling or even longer. On most of the routes, 10- or 12-speed touring bicycles are recommended. But mountain or hybrid bicycles can be used and are even recommended on the Kal-Haven Trail and the St. Joseph County route. The routes are a mixture of narrow roads with no shoulders, busy roadways with paved shoulders and bike paths through towns, woods, forests and open farm country. Most important, the tours are geared for sightseeing, and eating, not competitive racing. Shorter options are ideal for beginners or those who don't want to go a long distance.

The West Michigan region has been divided into three sections: Southwest, Central West and Northwest. Most of the routes list attractions that will be of interest to cyclists such as places to stop and eat, creative lodging ideas and bicycle shops in the area. The route descriptions and directions will give you an idea of the terrain while covering the unique aspects of each trip. Six of the routes (White Pine, Travese Area Recreation Trail, Kal-Haven, Hart-Montague, Musketawa and Kent Trails) are partially on converted rail beds, part of the growing rails-to-trails movement (see Appendix on page 215).

To develop the tours, I consulted bicycling clubs, studied state and county cycling maps and worked with local tourism officials before hitting the road and riding the routes. These are by no means the only cycling routes worth touring in West Michigan - we could probably provide you with 100 tours. But these are some of the very

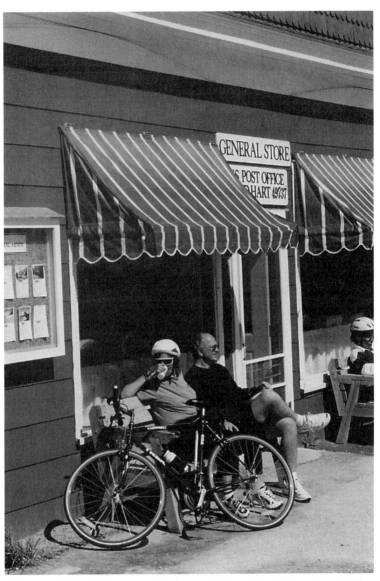

Two cyclists take a resfreshment break at the Good Hart General Store and Post Office during a ride along M-119 north of Harbor Springs.

best and provide an excellent taste of our beautiful region.

Climate

Changeable is the word that best describes weather in West Michigan. Although some cyclists chase their sport year-round, May through October are the most popular months to cycle in West Michigan. In May, or even earlier in April, showers are frequent but there are also pleasant stretches of weather when the skies are blue and temperatures are a comfortable 50 to 60 degrees. Wildflowers are emerging along roadsides at this time of year and best of all there are no bugs to stick to your teeth.

There is more traffic in West Michigan June through August, due to the region's popularity as a vacation designation. Temperatures at this time of year can range anywhere from a pleasant 70 degrees to a blistering 90 degrees. Sunny weather and clear skies are the norm but watch for sudden thunderstorms that rumble off Lake Michigan and across the state.

If you can get away, fall is an ideal time to cycle in West Michigan. From September through October temperatures return to those pleasant levels below 70 degrees. Showers are common (especially on the weekends it seems) but so are those glorious Indian summer days when the sky is azure blue, the air dry and the trees are peaking in their autumn hues of red, yellow and vivid orange. The hardwoods in West Michigan begin changing colors in mid-September and peak from the first week of October in areas around Petoskey, to the end of that month at the southwest corner.

Riding after October? Just make sure you wear your wool gloves and long underwear. Regardless of when you ride, always pack rain gear or at least a windbreaker, even if the sun is shining when you begin. You never know with Michigan weather!

Bicycle Safety

Bicycle helmets are strongly recommended whenever you go riding. Wearing a helmet can prevent serious head injuries and reduces (some experts say by as much as 85 percent) the chances of injuring yourself if you are thrown from your bicycle. Look for the CPSC or Snell sticker on the inside of the helmet. Although helmets can be expensive, they are a necessary investment for all cyclists.

Replacing Your Bicycle Helmet

According to the Bicycle Helmet Safety Institute one of the most common mistakes among cyclists is not replacing a dated helmet. Invest in a new helmet:

❏ Any time you crash.

Helmets protect your head with a foam liner that crushes on impact to absorb the blow. Every crash diminishes the impact protection of it .

❏ If a helmet is more than five years old.

Older helmets have been exposed to years of ultra violet and infra red light, exhaust fumes and sweat. All of these along with the usual wear and tear can affect the foam liner and its absorption ability.

❏ If its lacks a CPSC, ASTM or Snell sticker.

The tests today are much more rigorous for bicycle helmets than they were even three or four years ago.

❏ If it doesn't fit properly.

Push firmly on the helmet's front edge and if it moves up enough to expose the forehead, it's leaving you unprotected during a crash. Either re-adjust it or purchase a better fitting model.

❏ If it makes you look geeky.

If you're not comfortable with the way the helmet looks, you're not going to wear it. If that's the case, buy a flashier one.

Here are some other tips for a safe trip:

Safety check your bike: Before a tour, especially a long one, perform a quick inspection of your bicycle, paying close attention to your brakes, spokes, tires and quick release hubs. Make sure everything is operating smoothly to avoid an unexpected mishap on the road.

Ride with the flow of traffic: Do not ride against the flow of traffic and do not pull off the road every time a car approaches on narrow shoulders. Be careful: the transition between roadbed and shoulder is rarely smooth and can cause you to lose control.

Increase your visibility: Wear bright colored clothes and jackets instead of darker colors or earth tones to increase your visibility with motorists.

Pay attention to the road: There is a tendency at times to daydream while cycling long distances. It's easy to do as you fall into a rhythmic trance due to the constant motion of pedaling. But be alert for road signs, intersections, and patches of loose gravel, wet leaves or unexpected pot holes.

Observe all traffic signs: More times than not cycling accidents are caused by careless cyclists. Avoid coasting through stop signs or racing through yellow lights. Treat every intersection as if you were in a car.

Be prepared for bothersome dogs: Some bikers carry a spray can of dog repellent that can be purchased at any good bike shop. Others simply try to "outrun" the dog. Whatever, have a plan ready for when a snapping mutt is chasing you.

Packing For A Bike Tour

Always bring plenty of water. If there is any room in your bike bags after you've packed the other necessities (a dozen Hershey bars, boxes of fruit juice, a pound of trail mix, etc.) you might want to throw in a few tools. The four most common bike breakdowns on the roads are flat tires, broken brake cable, a suddenly wobbling wheel and an off-sprocket chain.

All four can be repaired at roadside if you have the right tools. At this point the Hershey bars are useless. Here's a list of suggested tools. Pack what the distance and number of days you'll be on the road dictate:

Crescent wrench: Don't ride anywhere without one. Useful to change a tire, adjust spokes and tighten any nut or bolt that comes loose.

Tire irons: Three plastic ones are lightweight and make changing a tire a lot easier.

Tube patch kit: Along with the kit, you should pack along a spare tube on longer rides.

Frame-mounted tire pump: How else are you going to inflate the spare or add some extra air to your tires?

Screwdrivers: Both a slot and a Phillips head type. Your best bet is to invest in a small tool kit from a bike shop designed to provide what you need when repairing your bike on the road or be easily stored in a compact case when you're not.

Small can of WD-40: It's nice to carry some lubrication along on those multi-day bike tours.

This and that: Depending on your bike model, you might want Allen wrenches, vise grip pliers and paper clips when all else fails. It's amazing what you can repair with a paper clip.

One more thing; either know how to make the necessary repairs, pack along the manual or ride with a friend who can. All the tools in the world are useless if you don't know what you're doing. In which case the dozen Hershey bars comes in handy...gives you something to do while waiting for help.

Karen's Favorites:

Every route in this book is special in its own way. To have some fun, I came up with these categories to serve as a further guide.

Most romantic: Saugatuck shorter option.

Best for kids: Hart-Montague Trail.

Best for large groups: Hart-Montague Trail or White Pine Trail.

Best workout for experienced cyclists: Sleeping Bear/Glen Lake.

Most scenic: Old Mission Peninsula.

Best lakeshore route: Ludington.

Best wooded inland: Kal-Haven Trail.

And finally the best gastronomical tour on a bicycle: Geez, I don't know, you can eat well on all of them...but the Torch Lake tour does wind past the best ice cream shops and eateries.

Happy Cycling!!!

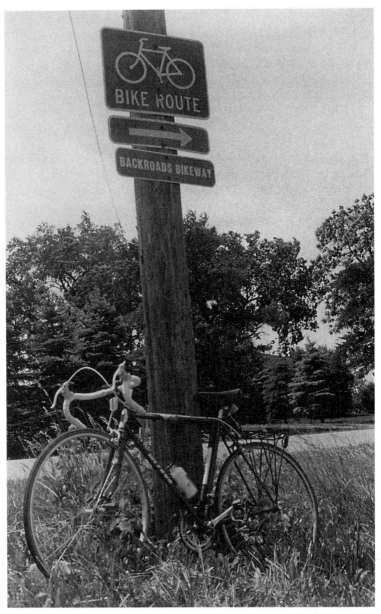

A Backroads Bikeway sign along the Lake Michigan Trail.

1 Lake Michigan Trail

Trip Card

Starting point: Three Oaks
County: Berrien
Distance: 31 miles
Shorter option: 8 miles
Terrain: mostly flat, some rolling hills
Highlights: Bicycle Museum, New
Buffalo, Lake Michigan, Warren Woods
Natural Area
Suggested riders: beginners to intermediate

Picture a small town in southwestern Michigan, near the Indiana border. It's a small town of under 2,000 residents; a quiet, pleasant community with an annual Flag Day Festival in June. Then, picture this same town with 7,000 cyclists converging on the area for the annual Apple Cider Century, happening at the end of September every year.

That's what you have in Three Oaks, Michigan, located 10 miles inland from Lake Michigan, five miles from the Indiana border and 20 miles from the St. Joseph/Benton Harbor area in southwestern Michigan. The Apple Cider Century is a one-day event, offering cyclists a choice of 25, 50, 75 or 100-mile rides through a variety of scenery; orchards, woods, vineyards, wineries, the Lake Michigan shoreline and pleasing small towns.

Since that rainy, cold day of the first Apple Cider Century in 1974, the event has grown to become the Midwest's biggest one-day century event. The annual event is sponsored by the Three Oaks Spokes Bicycle Club, a group of cycling enthusiasts from Indiana and Michigan. The Three Oaks area would have to be the bicycling mecca of West Michigan if one were named. Monies raised from the Apple Cider Century supports the popular Bicycle History Museum in the Michigan Central Railroad Depot on Oak Street in Three Oaks, and for signs and four-color brochures for the Backroads Bikeway, a system of 10 self-guided routes in the area. All the routes in the brochure, ranging from eight to 60 miles, begin at the Bicycle Museum. The routes are easy to follow with the brochure, and because of the green and white Backroads Bikeway signs throughout the system.

Bryan Volstorf, executive director of the museum, works year round to make sure the annual Apple Cider Century goes off without a hitch. The museum averages 8,000 to 10,000 visitors per year, not counting the visitors on the one-day Apple Cider Century. A variety of commemorative T-shirts and cycling accessories are also for sale at the museum and there's lots of free West Michigan travel information.

The Backroads Bikeway routes follow gurgling streams, open farm country, two state parks, Lake Michigan shoreline and numerous shady, wooded roads and farm markets. The routes in this and the next chapter were adapated from the tours listed in the Backroads Bikeway brochure.

The 31-mile circuit and the shorter eight-mile option head south out of Three Oaks. The longer loop heads south from the Bicycle Museum and west toward Lake Michigan, into the town of New Buffalo - a lakeside, resort community filled with dockominiums, condominiums, antique shops, restaurants and bars. It's a tourist town, especially popular with Chicagoans; New Buffalo is the first Michigan town along the big lake.

This route takes you through the Warren Woods Natural Area, a nice place to take a break and walk on the trails. The shorter eight-mile loop will give beginning cyclists a chance to see some of the countryside while their more adventurous friends and family members go for the distance.

Stage One (8.9 miles) Head south on Elm Street out of the town of Three Oaks. You will pass a couple of family restaurants as you cycle through downtown Three Oaks. Drier's Butcher Shop, on the right, is an old-fashioned butcher shop, a historic site in a centennial building that some say features the best homemade liverwurst in the Midwest. In less than a mile you will be in open country. Turn right on Forest Lawn Road at *Mile 1.8* to reach the large and scenic

Forest Lawn Cemetery within a half mile. The road twists and turns as you make your way to New Buffalo. The road then curves and becomes Maudlin Road. More twists, more trees. There's a nice shady area near *Mile 7* before you reach the corner of Maudlin Road and whittaker Street at *Mile 9*.

Stage Two (10.8 miles) From Maudlin Road, turn (north) right on Whittaker Street into downtown New Buffalo. Hungry?? There's plenty of places to eat here such as Oink's Ice Cream, Casey's Pub and Rosie's Restaurant. Turn right on Rivera Road, hugging the lakeshore to Lake Shore Road (Rivera Road ends at Lake Shore Road). From Lake Shore Road turn left on Red Arrow Highway at *Mile 16.4* where you'll pass a Backroads Bikeway sign to help point you in the right direction. Red Arrow Highway has some interesting

Cycling West Michigan

❀❀❀❀❀❀❀❀❀❀❀❀❀❀❀❀❀❀❀❀

Three Oaks Bicycle Museum

All Backroads Bikeway Routes begin and end at the Three Oaks Spokes Bicycle Museum where every cyclist should take a few minutes to enjoy its collection of vintage bikes. That includes an 1860 Velocipede, one of the earliest bicycles ever made, featuring two wheels, handlebars and a seat... but no rubber tires, inflated inner tubes or anything that resembled a spring or a wire spoke.

Thus its nickname; the Boneshaker.

"People look at that bike and leave thankful of what they have," said museum director Bryan Volstorf. "No matter what they're riding."

This unique museum in Berrien County is not only a place to see an 1893 Companion, a tandem bike where two people pedal side-by-side, but is also the trailhead to the 12 road routes and six Outback Trails for mountain bikers.

The increasing number of cyclists passing through town prompted the club to move its museum from a cramped storefront on Elm Street to the historic Michigan Central Railroad Depot in 1994.

The century old depot, featuring tin ceilings, beveled leaded glass windows and handcrafted copper light fixtures, was called "the finest depot between Niles and Chicago" in its heyday. Along with two exhibit rooms displaying 22 classic bicycles, the museum also serves as an information center, promoting Michigan and Indiana tourist attractions as well as cycling events and trails throughout the state.

The collection of ancient two-wheelers attracts cyclists into Three Oaks while the suggested routes give them a reason to stick around for the afternoon. You can even rent a bicycle at the museum or a bugger trailer to carry your toddlers in.

The Three Oaks Spokes Bicycle Museum is on Oak Street a block off Elm Street (Main Street). Hours are 9 a.m. to 5 p.m. daily and admission is free. For a map of the Backroads Bikeway or list of bicycle events call the museum at ☎ (616) 756-3361.

❀❀❀❀❀❀❀❀❀❀❀❀❀❀❀❀❀❀❀❀

Two cyclists end their ride at the Three Oaks Spokes Bicycle Museum, housed in the old Michigan Central Railroad Depot.

options for a break including an antique mall, and Capozios Pizza near *Mile 17.* You'll pass through the village of Harbert at *Mile 17.3* (don't blink or you'll miss it!). Turn right on Harbert Road within a quarter mile, cross Three Oaks Road and then turn right on Flynn Road at *Mile 19.7.*

Stage Three: (10.9 miles) Flynn Road is a narrow country road. A hilly stretch is reached at *Mile 20.4* followed by open country. Turn right on Warren Woods Road at *Mile 21.7.* Ceasar's Too is on the corner of Three Oaks Road and Warren Woods Road, a good place for pop or a candy bar. A long hill follows as the route curves to the right at *Mile 23.4* and travels through the Warren Woods Natural Area. Bob-A-Ron Campground, with 190 modern sites and 125 primitive sites, is on your left at *Mile 24.3.* Turn left on Lakeside Road at *Mile 25.8* and within a half mile you pass over I-94. At *Mile 26.7* turn left on Kruger Road, a level road through open countryside. Turn right on Three Oaks Road at *Mile 30.6* and in a short jaunt you'll be back at the Bicycle Museum and the starting point.

Shorter option (8 miles) From the Bicycle Museum, head south on Elm Street (Three Oaks Road) to Forest Lawn Road; turn right. Travel Forest Lawn Road to Basswood Road and turn left (south). Ride to Martin Road; turn left (east). Take Martin Road back to Three Oaks Road. Turn left here and head into downtown Three Oaks and back to your starting point at the Bicycle Museum.

Bicycle sales, service

Cycle Path, 5684 St. Joseph Ave., Stevensville; ☎ (616) 429-4483.

Baker's Bike Shop Inc., 135 Dixie Way South, South Bend, IN; ☎ (219) 277-8866.

Area events and festivals

June: Flag Day Festival, Three Oaks.

September: Apple Cider Century, Three Oaks; Four Flags Area Apple Festival, Niles.

Area attractions

Fernwood Nature Center, Niles; ☎ (616) 683-8653.

Tabor Hill Winery & Restaurant, Buchanan; ☎ (616) 422-1161.

Cook Energy Information Center, Bridgman; ☎ (616) 465-6101 or (800) 548-2555.

Travel information

Backroads Bikeway, 110 N. Elm St., Three Oaks, MI 49128; ☎ (616) 756-3361 (SASE for free Backroads Bikeway brochure).

Harbor Country Chamber of Commerce, New Buffalo; ☎ (616) 469-5409 or (800) 362-7251, *www.harborcountry.org*.

The Southwestern Michigan Tourist Council, Benton Harbor, ☎ (616) 925-6301, *www.swmichigan.org*.

2 Grand Mere Dunes

Trip Card

Starting point: Grand Mere State Par
County: Berrien
Distance: 50 miles
Shorter option: 17 miles
Terrain: mostly flat, some rolling hills
Highlights: Grand Mere and Warren Dunes state parks, vineyards
Suggested riders: intermediate, beginners for shorter loop

Grand Mere was designated a state park in 1973, but it wasn't until the 1990's that a portion of the park's master plan was implemented. It used to be an area known only by locals and residents who summered there, including Chicago celebrities, with many wanting the dunes and three small lakes to remain a well-kept secret. Slowly the rest of the state is discovering the lakeshore beauty of Grand Mere.

The park features a shelter, hiking trails, sand dunes, varied land formations and flora, not to mention an easily accessible parking area, which makes it a good starting point for this 50-mile route. Most of all, Grand Mere is blessed with a beautiful, wide sandy beach on Lake Michigan, an ideal place to cool off after any bike tour in the summer. Grand Mere is also only seven miles from downtown St. Joseph, which offers an array of shopping, a kids' museum, art center and numerous restaurants.

These two routes were adapted from the Backroads Bikeway brochure, developed by the Three Oaks Spokes Bicycle Club. The longer route begins at Grand Mere State Park, near Stevensville, a bedroom community to the St. Joseph and Benton Harbor area.

Cycling West Michigan

From Grand Mere, the ride heads south toward the better known and more developed Warren Dunes State Park, that features a large modern campground as well as an impressive beach of its own. This 50-mile circuit then makes its way toward Three Oaks, traveling past Warren Woods Natural Area, open farmland and then through downtown Three Oaks, the only town in Michigan with a Bicycle Museum (see page 26). The terrain on this route is varied enough to delight most cyclists and includes wide open roads, stretches of shaded pavement and a couple of small towns. Baroda is "Smalltown, U.S.A." little more than a V-shaped intersection, 1,000 residents, and a few places to eat (or drink!) that attracts more than just those who call Baroda home.

The 50-mile route and the 17-mile shorter option offer cyclists variety with a capital "V". Where else could you find Lake Michigan shoreline, two state parks, lush farmfields, vineyards, a bicycle museum and a century old butcher shop (downtown Three Oaks) that appears to have changed little since opening in 1875.

Stage one (16.6 miles) From the entrance of Grand Mere State Park, head south on Thornton Road as it curves and winds past the forested state park. At *Mile 2.8* you'll reach Livingston Road where you turn left and cross Red Arrow Highway. ⚠ *Caution: Red Arrow can be busy in the summer and fall.* At *Mile 3.8* turn right on Jericho Road, a level ride through scenic, open country. You'll pass Lemon Creek Road and the Pebblewood Country Club and Golf Course and at Snow Road you've pedalled seven miles. Turn right.

Snow Road makes a couple of curves in the next two miles, the second time while you're heading downhill. At *Mile 10.5*, turn right on Browntown Road, and then turn left on Flynn Road a mile later. You'll struggle up a steep hill at *Mile 12* and then pass a picturesque church on the corner of Flynn and Sawyer roads within a half mile. Flynn becomes somewhat bumpy, then turns into a delightful downhill stretch through a shady area followed by an uphill ride at *Mile 14.2*. At Flynn and Warren Woods Road, you've gone 15.6 miles; turn right on Warren Woods Road. Time for your first break or a candy bar.

Stage two (8.9 miles) From the Three Oaks Road intersection, continue heading west (left) on Warren Woods Road. In less than a mile, you'll be cycling through the Warren Woods Natural Area and past a posted trailhead. This 300-acre preserve is actually a part of Warren Dunes State Park and represents one of the last virgin climax beech-maple forests in the state. The trail is a 2-mile loop to the Galien River. Even if that's too much hiking on your day to bike, just wander a hundred yards down the wooded path and you'll see virgin beech so large that two people can't link their arms around them. This gorgeous shaded area is great for a weather-beaten cyclist sizzled by a hot August afternoon.

Warren Woods Road curves a bit to the right as you leave the natural area and head into a residential section. At *Mile 18.2*, the Bob-A-Ron Campground is on your left (canoeing, fishing, swimming, plus modern and primitive sites). From there it's uphill and over I-94 where below you will be the summer snarl of travelers rushing off to their "vacation," and at *Mile 19.7* you turn left on Lakeside Road, a road that's narrow, but well shaded. Lakeside also involves a couple of long uphill climbs before you turn left on Kruger Road at *Mile 21.5*. After a stretch of scenic rolling farm fields, turn right on Three Oaks Road at *Mile 24.5* and look south for Three Oaks' skyline in the distance. You won't see one because this homey village of of less than 2,000 doesn't have one. What it does have, appearing soon on your left, is the world famous (okay, how about Midwest famous) Bicycle Museum (see page 26) at *Mile 25.3*. The museum is in downtown Three Oaks, where there are several options for a short or longer rest. The museum itself has picnic tables for cyclists, or there are a couple of family restaurants, historic Drier's Butcher Shop and a gas station/convenience store for a smorgasbord of junk food at *Mile 25.5*.

Stage three (19 miles) From downtown Three Oaks, backtrack by heading north on Three Oaks Road to Kruger Road; turn right. Kruger Road is a road with picturesque farmland typical of this rural corner of the state. Near *Mile 29* turn left on Mill Road and go two miles to Warren Woods Road; turn right. Travel east for a mile, cross the Galien River and then immediately turn left onto Log Cabin Road, a narrow road that features a one-lane bridge. At *Mile 34.4* turn right on Glendora Road where you cycle past the seen-better-days Lintner Tavern, a white clapboard structure, before entering the hamlet of Glendora. After a couple of rolling hills, turn left (north) on Hills Road, which is a slightly bumpy but shaded roadway. Smell the air, and savor the aroma as you cycle through vineyards at *Mile 40.3*. A long hill is encountered at *Mile 41.5* and then the road curves sharply to the right and you'll pass Heart of the Vineyard Bed & Breakfast (☎ 616-422-1617) at *Mile 42*.

In less than a half mile from the bed and breakfast, Hills Road merges into Snow Road and then immediately veers to the right (and later becomes Stevensville/Baroda Road). Stay on Hill Road and at *Mile 43.6* you'll pass an arrow pointing to Lemon Creek Winery and

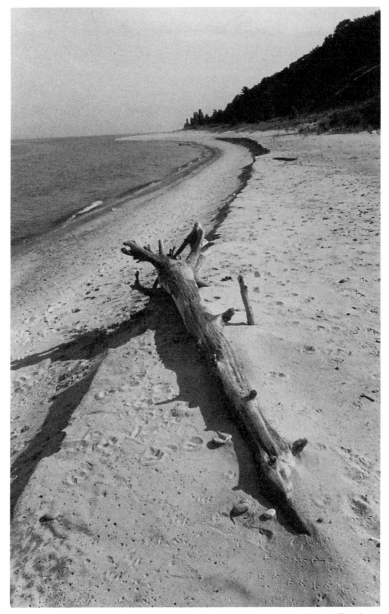

The Lake Michigan beach at Grand Mere State Park.

Fruits & Veggies In Southwest Michigan

Berrien and Van Buren counties in Michigan lead the state and even the nation when it comes to the production of some fruits and vegetables. The two counties grow more than 40,000 acres of fruit with 14,000 acres devoted to Michigan apples from the well known Red Delicious variety to lesser known Honeycrisp, Jonagold and Winesap.

What does this mean to touring cyclists? All this fruit and veggie growing means there's lots of farm markets and even agricultural entertainment such as pumpkin patches and corn mazes. In this region you'll find baked apple pies in a paper bag at a farm market, 10 pounds of fresh blueberries for $10 or the first sweet corn on the market, often available as early as the Fourth of July and picked fresh every day.

Fruit Farms (☎ 616-471-1321), a family-owned vineyard, offering winery tours and opportunities to pick fruit in season from their orchards. At *Mile 44.5* you'll arrive at Baroda, a Centennial community with a population of only 657. Baroda is rural Americana, with red, white and blue banners waving to you as you ride through town. Need a break? You will soon pass on your left Connie's Place and Bill's Tap, two bar/restaurants.

Stage Four (5.8 miles) The last part of the journey leads out of Baroda and heads toward Stevensville. Continue cycling on Stevensville-Baroda Road and at *Mile 46* you'll cross Cleveland Avenue, a very busy four-way intersection. There's a "Welcome to Stevensville" sign just before *Mile 49* and within a half mile you'll be in downtown Stevensville, a small lakeshore community. Here Stevensville-Baroda Road becomes St. Joseph Avenue and you turn left on John Beers Road to head west toward Lake Michigan. Cycle Path Bike Shop is located in downtown Stevensville. Cross Red Arrow Highway, a busy intersection at *Mile 49.8*, and at this point John Beers Road turns into a long, downhill. ⚠ *Caution: the road curves to the right and you will still need to watch for cars on this lightly traveled road as you careen down the steep hill.* Turn left on Thornton Drive and at *Mile 50.3*, you're back to the entrance to Grand Mere State Park. Relax, it's time to stretch those legs, look for rare plants, do dune climbing or just spread out on the beach and recuperate.

Shorter option (17 miles) From Bicycle Museum in downtown Three Oaks, head north on Three Oaks Road to Kruger Road; turn right. Cycle on Kruger Road to Mill Road; turn left (north). Follow the Backroads Bikeway signs. Turn left on Warren Woods Road through Warren Woods Natural Area to Lakeside Road. Turn left (south) on Lakeside, back to Kruger Road and turn left (east). Travel east on Kruger Road to Three Oaks Road where you turn right (south) and return to the Bicycle Museum.

Bicycle sales, service
Cycle Path, 5684 St. Joseph, Stevensville; ☎ (616) 429-4483.

Cycle & Fitness, 2621 Niles Avenue, St. Joseph; ☎ (616) 983-2453.

Area events and festivals
June: Flag Day, Three Oaks.

July: Discover Stevensville Festival, Stevensville.

Late September: Apple Cider Century, Three Oaks.

Area attractions
Bicycle Museum, One Oak St., Three Oaks; ☎ (616) 756-3361.

Lemon Creek Winery, Berrien Springs; ☎ (616) 471-1321.

Cook Energy Information Center, Bridgman; ☎ (800) 548-2555.

Travel information
The Southwestern Michigan Tourist Council, Benton Harbor; ☎ (616) 925-6301, *www.swmichigan.org*.

Harbor Country Chamber of Commerce, New Buffalo; ☎ (616) 469-5409 or (800) 326-7251, *www.harborcountry.org*.

Sister Lakes

Trip Card

Starting point: Wicks Apple House
Location: Cass, Van Buren counties
Distance: 14.5 miles
Shorter option: 4.5 miles
Terrain: flat, some slight hills
Highlights: Wicks' Apple House,
 Dewey Lake, Magician Lake, Little
 Crooked Lake, Big Crooked Lake, Round Lake
Suggested riders: beginners

The first thing cyclists need to know about this loop is that Sister Lakes doesn't exist. That is, Sister Lakes is not a body of water, but a town, situated near a series of six lakes. This 14.5-mile bicycle route ambles around these lakes in a tour that touches two southwestern Michigan counties - Van Buren and Cass - while being very close to Berrien County. It's a short circuit that starts at Wicks' Apple House, a relaxing restaurant with great lunches and a produce market, bakery and cider mill. The best season for this route is the fall to see the apple harvest at Wicks, and the autumn palette of colors reflected in the waters of this easily accessible region.

Sister Lakes is a mere 90 miles from Chicago, and 30 miles from South Bend, Indiana. It's also close to the St. Joseph/Benton Harbor area and Kalamazoo in southwestern Michigan. The resort area has attracted visitors since 1876 when Nelson Decker opened a blacksmith shop and made an all-day horse and buggy trip to Benton Harbor to meet the ferry from Chicago. Crooked Lake, one of the six lakes, even had an excursion steamboat operating until 1903.

Today the Sister Lakes area is a low-key resort area, with unpretentious cottages and resorts featuring small cabins on the lakes. In summer, there's lots of boating and swimming on the water, probably because these lakes are warmer than Lake Michigan.

This route could easily be combined with the Three Oaks Backroads Bikeway routes, described earlier, for a weekend outing. The loop winds around several of the lakes in this area and at one point you cycle between two lakes, the 110-acre Big Crooked Lake and the 103-acre Little Crooked Lake. This stretch provides the unusual ride of gliding past the two bodies of water as if you were on a bridge.

The Sister Lakes tour also includes the Sacred Heart of Mary Catholic Church, an old mission church with an equally interesting cemetery featuring gravestones dating back to the mid-1800s. This scenic country church is a Michigan historic site and attracts so many vacationers during the summer that an outdoor pavilion was built.

There are several small-town places to eat. Try the Driftwood Summer Shop near Sister Lakes for hand-dipped ice creams (including my favorite, Mackinac Island Fudge!) or the Country Corner Coffee Shop and Frosty Delighton Highway 152 in town. Four miles from Wicks' Apple House, is another orchard stop, Tree-Mendus Fruit Farm on Eureka Road in Eau Claire. Owners Herb and Liz Teichman know how to make families and large groups feel welcome with shaded picnic areas, restrooms, orchard tours and sun-ripened fruits in season. In July, the fruit farm conducts the annual Cherry Pit Spitting competition that attracts contestants from all over the country. Patooey!

Stage One (9.5 miles) Start from Wicks' Apple House located at 52281 Indian Lake road near the corner of Silver Street in the extreme northwestern corner of Cass County. Cycle north on Indian Lake Road and then turn right on Topash Street in a third of a mile. This narrow road is lightly travelled and passes vineyards, cornfields and red raspberry farms within the first mile. After passing through a residential section turn left onto Leach Road at the stop sign at *Mile 3.3.* Just ahead on your right is the historic Sacred Heart of Mary Catholic Church with a cemetery on a hill. In 1838, Chief Leopold Pokagon of the Potawatomi Indians built a log church here on what was then an old Indian graveyard. Eventually he deeded the 40 acres of land to the Catholic bishop of Detroit and in 1844 Father Theophile Marifault became the church's first permanent priest.

Louis Baroux followed, served from 1847-1879, and was buried in the cemetery in 1897. Also buried here in 1841 was Chief Pokagon.

The tour continues from the historic church down a moderate hill at *Mile 3.8*. You'll cycle past a variety of orchards, including cherries, as well as more cornfields. At *Mile 4.4* turn left on M-152, a hilly road that can be busy in the summer but is relatively wide with gravel shoulders. You'll enjoy a mixture of residential homes and rolling cornfields before tackling another uphill stretch at *Mile 5.5*, highlighted by a faded red barn, and then a downhill run curving sharply to your right. The road twists and curves but provides good views of Dewey Lake on the left followed by an uphill segment at *Mile 6*.

Within a half mile turn left on Garrett Road as it continues to skirt the shoreline of Dewey Lake. A lot of boaters and water skiers will be seen on the water during the summer before you enter the shaded relief of a tunnel of trees.

Just beyond *Mile 7* turn right on Dixon Road, another well shaded stretch of pavement, and continue straight on the road after stopping for the intersection with Indian Lake Road at *Mile 7.7*. Just beyond, there is a scenic cemetery and then Dixon Road curves to the right and becomes Sister Lakes Road. More apple and cherry orchards are passed as you follow the winding Sister Lakes Road north. This stretch is level and is a leisurely ride past views of Little Crooked Lake. You enter Van Buren County near *Mile 9* followed by an uphill segment that curves sharply to your right within view of Round Lake. The road then curves left and just ahead at *Mile 9.5* is the Driftwood Summer Shop, offering T-shirts, souvenirs, beach supplies, and of course, ice cream. Time to take a break, stretch those legs and enjoy a sweet treat! There are more food choices in Sister Lakes; just cycle north on Sister Lake Road to reach the small town and add more distance to this circuit.

Stage Two (5 miles) From Driftwood Summer Shop take a right on 95th Avenue where there is a directional arrow. This stretch of 95th Avenue is a narrow road that twists and curves between Little Crooked and Big Crooked lakes, which at one time was a single body of water. These lakes are the highlight of this lakeshore amble as you'll be almost surrounded by water. At *Mile 9.7* the road curves to the left and climbs a small hill. Turn right at M-152 at *Mile 10.5* to quickly enter Cass County. After passing a hot dog and ice cream stand (time for another break?) at *Mile 11.3*, you turn right on Garrett

Road and repeat an earlier segment of the road.

With Dewey Lake on your left, you'll cycle past the Shady Shores Resort at *Mile 12.3*. The resort features cottages, trailer sites and a beach and recreational area. From Shady Shores it's a few more curves past more swaying cornfields to reach Topash Street at *Mile 13.2*. Backtrack along Topash and turn left on Indian Lake Road at *Mile 14.2* to reach Wicks' Apple House in less than a third of a mile. Time to browse for gifts at Wicks', purchase cider for the trip home, or sample one of their many tasty desserts!

Shorter option (4.5 miles) From Wicks' Apple House, cycle north on Indian Lake Road and turn right on Topash Street. Follow with a left on Garrett Road and then another left on Dixon Road. Finish the short route by turning left on Indian Lake Road and cycling back to Wicks' Apple House.

Bicycle sales, service

Baker's Bike Shop Inc., 135 Dixie Way S., South Bend, Indiana; ☎ (219) 277-8866.

Cycle & Fitness, 2621 Niles Avenue, St. Joseph; ☎ (616) 983-2453.

Area events and festivals

June: Fishing Contest, Sister Lakes.

July: Doe-Waj-Jack Fun Festival, Dowagiac; International Cherry Pit Spitting Championship, Eau Claire; Fourth of July fireworks, Lions Park, Sister Lakes.

September: Flirt with Fall Fest, Sister Lakes.

October: Ciderfest, Wicks' Apple House, Dowagiac.

Area attractions

Wicks' Apple House, Dowagiac; ☎ (616) 782-7306.

Tree-Mendus Fruit Farm, Eau Claire; ☎ (616) 782-7101.

Travel information

Southwestern Michigan Tourist Council; ☎ (616) 925-6301, *www.swmichigan.org*.

Blossomland

Trip Card

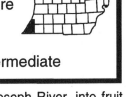

Starting point: St. Joseph
County: Berrien
Distance: 28 miles
Terrain: mostly flat, some hills
Highlights: Herb Barn, Sarett Nature
Center, Lake Michigan, Curious
Kids Museum
Suggested riders: beginner to intermediate

From Lake Michigan, across the St. Joseph River, into fruit growing farms in Benton Township and back to the lakeshore again, cyclists will find this 28-mile route that circles the St. Joseph/Benton Harbor area a pleasant journey.

This route will underscore the best of what southwestern Michigan has to offer; beautiful beaches, terrific shopping, lush fruit growing areas, parks and country backroads. Plan to spend the entire day. There's a place to pause and relax at each of the four stages. This route begins near downtown St. Joseph, which has enjoyed a renaissance. Whether you're looking for antiques, gourmet popcorn, educational toys, a kite to fly at the beach or a colorful windsock, you can find it in downtown St. Joseph. Most of the shops are located on State Street, a quaint red brick road. A block west and running parallel to State Street is Lake Boulevard, bordering a park located on a bluff overlooking Lake Michigan, the site of St. Joseph's annual art fair every July.

All-day parking can be found between Lake Boulevard on the bluff and along the 400 block of State Street. You can't miss the parking lot, it's next to the Curious Kids Museum. Be sure to begin or end your ride with a visit to this fun hands-on museum. Next stop: the Herb Barn in Benton Township. Everything for growing, enjoying or sharing herb lore is sold in the "barn," which is surrounded by a greenhouse and many demonstration herb gardens.

The third stage of the trip rambles through orchards, farmlands, and gently rolling hills, where roadside vegetable stands offer the bounty of the season. There are lots of fruits and vegetables grown in the area with something always ripe and ready to eat. Plan a stop at the scenic Sarett Nature Center for an extended rest, a walk in the woods, or to do a little birding. Bikes are not allowed on the Sarett trails, but you can stretch your legs with a stroll to the Paw Paw River.

Another highlight on this route is a heart-pounding, twisting ride down Rocky Gap Road through a canopy of trees, perched high alongside Lake Michigan. Rocky Gap Park, with a scenic overlook is an ideal final stopover before heading back to St. Joseph. Along with enjoying the overlook, you can also walk down the dunes to a sandy Lake Michigan beach to sunbathe in summer or watch the lapping waves on a crisp fall afternoon. If you didn't "go jump in the lake" at Rocky Gap, you can at St. Joseph's Silver Beach. Even if you enjoyed a hearty picnic lunch along the way, you'll be glad to know that downtown St. Joseph has plenty of fine eating establishments. Schu's Grill & Bar, on Lake Boulevard, and Roxy's (known for its burgers) at the train depot, near Silver Beach, offer outdoor dining for the cyclist who just can't bear to be indoors after a ride.

Stage One (6.7 miles) From Lake Boulevard in downtown St. Joseph, go east (right) on Broad Street. You will cross busy Main Street in a quarter mile and then curve right where Broad Street becomes Langley Avenue. Pass Clementine's Restaurant (a nice restaurant on the St. Joseph River) on your left in a half mile and Kiwanis Park, a city park, a quarter mile down the road before turning left on Napier Avenue at *Mile 1.6*. In a quarter mile, you'll reach the St. Joseph River. ⚠ *Walk your bike across the bridge and be alert as the traffic can often be heavy here.*

Continue on Napier Avenue to Colfax Avenue; turn right. Turn left on Nickerson Avenue at *Mile 3.4* and continue biking past M-139, which can be a busy intersection most times. Take the right fork and then turn at the first left after the expressway overpass. Follow this road around the curve onto Townline Road. At *Mile 5.6* take a left on Pipestone Road and then turn right on Meadowbrook Road, where located across the street is the Southwestern Michigan Tourist Council headquarters, a great place for area information (maps, brochures). There's also a Bob Evans restaurant and an expressway ramp which makes this a busy corner. ⚠ *Be careful!*

Just up Meadowbrook Road at *Mile 6.5* into tour, turn left onto Greenley Road for your first stop: The Herb Barn (☎ 616-927-2044). This scenic barn has been converted into an indoor/outdoor shop selling herbs, plants, planters, candles, seasonal decorations, seeds, garden supplies, etc. This is a wonderfully sweet-smelling shopping and a learning experience - worth a lengthy visit.

Stage Two (7.1 miles) From the Herb Barn, backtrack a quarter mile to Meadowbrook Road and turn left (east). Near *Mile 8* turn left onto Yore Avenue and head north to Napier Avenue where at *Mile 8.6* you turn right, just past Lake Michigan College. Go east on Napier Avenue for a half mile and then turn left (north) on Benton Center Road near *Mile 9*. This road passes through a flat stretch of open country where picturesque farms and vineyards make it an exhilarating stretch for the cyclist. You cross Empire Avenue near *Mile 10*. Continue north and at *Mile 13.8* you'll reach Sarett Nature Center (☎ 616-927-4832), your second stop.

Sarett Nature Center is a 400-acre preserve for viewing wildlife in its natural habitat. There's an excellent exhibit area, five miles of walking trails, glassed-in viewing areas and a gift shop for nature lovers. Sarett also has a nice spot for a picnic lunch.

Stage Three (4.2 miles) From the nature center, turn left (north) on Benton Center Road which quickly becomes Schmuhl Road. Part of Schmuhl is gravel, so those with road bikes may want to walk their bikes and push them up the hill. The road is still gravel as it descends through a tunnel of trees at *Mile 14.4*. Within a third of a mile, gravel turns to pavement as Schmuhl curves east. This uphill ride is followed by another long, gradual ascent at *Mile 15*. Just past the expressway overpass, take a left (north) on Kerlikowski Road at *Mile 15.4*, where you will cycle by some of the orchards that make Southwest Michigan a cornucopia of fruit. Continue north until you reach Coloma Road near *Mile 17* where you turn left (west). This road can be busy but you depart it within a mile at the next right (south), which is Riverside Road, to enter Riverside. In this small town, on the corner of Fikes and Riverside, you will find a grocery store called Handy Spot. This red and white building with an outside bench has small-town appeal and is a great place for refreshments and a short break.

Stage Four (10 miles) From Moore's, head southwest on Riverside Road. This road angles south and west toward Lake Michigan and along the way you'll cycle over railroad tracks, past the Riverside Post Office and through scenic stretches of open country, orchards and a stand of hardwood trees. Riverside Road ends at Paw Paw Avenue where you take a sharp right on Paw Paw Avenue and then an immediate left on Benson Road at *Mile 22.4*.

Continue west on Benson Road until it ends at M-63. Turn left on M-63 at *Mile 23* and follow the highway south along another busy stretch of road. Be patient, it doesn't last long. At *Mile 23.7* you turn

A cyclist enjoys the flowering orchards during a ride along the Blossomland Tour.

right from M-63 onto Rocky Gap Road. While a bit hilly, this road is the highlight of the day for many because of the canopy of trees that shade the road and the scenic views of Lake Michigan. Rocky Gap twists while staying within view of Lake Michigan most of the time. There is a panoramic lookout of Lake Michigan at 24.4 miles.

Turn right at Higman Park Road at 24.9 miles. Follow this road around the curve until it ends at Klock Road and turn right onto the one-way street. Soon Klock becomes Upton Drive and you continue south as the road curves sharply to your left and up a hill to the Blossomland Bridge. Although St. Joseph doesn't have a spectacular skyline, a water tower, historic Whitcomb Hotel and a church steeple to tell you there's a small, pleasing city just ahead.

At the top of the hill there's a traffic light. Turn right and ⚠ *walk your bike across the bridge.* To reach Silver Beach Park, turn right again at the next traffic light at *Mile 26.7* and then turn right at a three-way stop sign (Water Street) and descend a steep hill, following the St. Joseph River to its mouth on Lake Michigan. Roxy's, located in the old St. Joseph train depot, will be on your left. The road curves sharply to your right and ends at Lake Michigan, near Silver Beach, at *Mile 27.2*. The name of this road changes from Water Street to Vine Street to Broad Street, although it is not as confusing as it sounds. Just look toward Lake Michigan and you won't get lost.

Backtrack the way you came, up the steep hill curving to your right to reach Lake Boulevard. The St. Joseph bandshell, where free concerts are hosted throughout the summer, is on your right at *Mile 27.7*. Turn left on Lake Boulevard. Schu's (for outdoor dining) is on your left at *Mile 27.8* and the bluff overlooking Lake Michigan is to your right. You are back to the starting point near the Curious Kids Museum at *Mile 28*. Time to visit the museum, sit on a bench overlooking Lake Michigan, or dine at a St. Joseph restaurant.

Bicycle sales, service
Cycle & Fitness, 2621 Niles Avenue, St. Joseph; ☎ (616) 983-2453.

Area events and festivals
May: Blossomtime Festival, Benton Harbor, St. Joseph.
July: St. Joseph Art Fair; Venetian Festival, St. Joseph.
September: Tri-State Regatta Festival, St. Joseph.

Area attractions
The Herb Barn, Benton Harbor; ☎ (616) 927-2044.
Sarett Nature Center, Benton Harbor; ☎ (616) 927-4832.
Curious Kids Museum, St. Joseph; ☎ (616) 983-2543.

Travel information
Southwestern Michigan Tourist Council, ☎ (616) 925-6301, *www.swmichigan.org*.
St. Joseph Today, ☎ (616) 982-0032, *www.sjtoday.org*.

5 Amish Tour

Trip Card

Starting point: Centreville
County: St. Joseph
Distance: 23.3 miles
Shorter option: 15 miles
Terrain: very flat, some gravel, loose surface roads on longer loop.
Highlights: Langley Covered Bridge, Amish farms, Lake Templene, St. Joseph River
Suggested riders: beginners to intermediate

Cyclists are naturally drawn to covered bridges, probably because there are so few of these nostalgic structures left in Michigan. The Langley Covered Bridge, built in 1887, is definitely the highlight of this 23-mile bicycle route that begins in Centreville. It is best to ride this route on a mountain or hybrid bicycle because some of the roads are gravel or loose textured.

The 23-mile route and the 15-mile shorter option are mostly flat. Traveling unpaved roads, cyclists will be inspired by the simplicity of the Amish people who live in this country setting. On Sunday afternoons, many Amish family members can be seen in buggies with horses trotting along at a slower speed than the slowest cyclist in your group! No electrical lines lead into their simple farm homes. The bright orange safety reflectors on the back of their buggies stand out in contrast to their dark, 19th century-style clothing. This ride will soothe the nerves of city dwellers as it winds through wooded areas, cornfields (after all, St. Joseph County is just north of LaGrange County, Indiana, a state where corn is king), man-made Lake Templene, residential homes and the placid St. Joseph River.

Your cares will evaporate into the country air when you realize that the only decision to be made in an afternoon of cycling here is whether to eat at the Lindy's in Centreville, grab a sandwich and candy bar at the Village Market, or tackle a pizza or sandwich at Angelo's Pizza & Subs at the starting point in Centreville. On the shorter loop, you might have to decide on a flavor of Hudsonville ice cream at the Sand Lake Ice Cream and Party Store in the small town of Nottawa.

St. Joseph County is sometimes overlooked when people search for a perfect weekend getaway or a fun, one-day outing. The small towns, waterways, bed & breakfast establishments, entertaining festivals and canoeing and biking opportunities make this accessible county a unique destination; one of those quiet surprises!

Today, the sleepy town of Colon, in the eastern part of the county, is home to the Abbott's Magic Manufacturing Co. (☎ 616-432-3235) which builds 2,000 magic tricks and gadgets. Every August, amateur and professional magicians congregate in the village for a series of shows at the high school auditorium. Magical memorabilia can be seen at the Colon Community Museum.

Stage One (3.9 miles) Beginning at Village Market parking lot in Centreville, turn left on M-86. At *Mile 0.8* turn right (north) onto Covered Bridge Road. You will soon be cycling through a mix of woodlands and open country. ⚠ *Caution: This is also Amish country and cyclists need to respect their horses and buggies on the road as they often move along at a slower pace.* Never accidentally spook a horse. Let them know what you are going to do or that you are approaching them. If they see you early they will rarely bolt. Remember, gently speak to horses, but never touch them without asking permission from the owner first.

Covered Bridge Road is a paved, flat road with no shoulders that near *Mile 4* crosses the St. Joseph River on the Langley Covered Bridge. At 282 feet, the structure is the longest covered bridge in Michigan and one of the heaviest at three tons. Built in 1887, the Langley Bridge had to be raised eight feet to avoid the surging waters when the Sturgis Dam was completed in 1910.

Nearby is Covered Bridge Park, a 15-acre park that features tables, grills and a good view of the historic bridge. Take a short break at this scenic spot if for no other reason than to rearrange your gear for the rest of the tour.

Stage Two (10.3 miles) Just south of the covered bridge, turn

Prairie Corners Rd.

8.1 Miles

N. Angling Rd.

Butler Rd.

Schweitzer Rd.

Covered Bridge Rd.

Angevine Rd.

Bucknell Rd.

Short loop · 15 Miles

Start · 0 Miles

Finish · 23.3 Miles

Truckenmiller Rd.

12.2 Miles

CENTREVILLE

Rambadt Rd.

86

NOTTAWA

Nottawa Rd.

Findley Rd.

Shimmel Rd.

Sauger Lake Rd.

20.7 Miles

N

right (east) on Schweitzer Road. This is an unpaved road that passes through a mixture of hardwood trees and cultivated fields - a great road for a mountain bike! The pavement returns when you turn left (north) on Angevine Road and then immediately turn right (east) on Butler Road at *Mile 5.2*. This road is paved at first and then becomes a stretch of gravel through more hardwoods and abundant farmfields. At *Mile 6.6* turn left (north) on North Angling, another gravel road that leads to more scattered forested areas in a third of a mile, and then turn right on paved Prairie Corners Road at *Mile 7.7*.

Turn right (south) on Bucknell Road just beyond *Mile 8*, a gravel road that heads south past Amish farms with horses and windmills, but not a single power line - a rather amazing sight in our day and age. Eventually you cycle over a one-lane bridge and a few rolling hills before turning right (west) on Truckenmiller Road at *Mile 12.2*, another gravel road. This road curves sharply to your left at *Mile 12.7* past Evans Lake, and then sharply to your right. Finish the second stage by turning left on Rambadt Road at *Mile 13.3*.

Stage Three (10 miles) Keep cycling south on Rambadt Road across M-86 near *Mile 14*. This portion of the road is paved and when it curves to your left, it becomes Findley Road. Findley curves around Lake Templene at *Mile 14.3*, a man-made lake that was created when small streams in the area were dammed. At *Mile 14.5* there are good views of Lake Templene to your right just before the road curves sharply south through a pleasant residential area and small farms near the lake. The road continues to wind past the lake, agricultural fields and at one point a picturesque, faded white barn, with noisy roosters in the barnyard. At *Mile 17* turn right (south) on Nottawa Road and within a half mile right (west) on Sauger Lake Road. This is a paved road with a pleasant mix of trees and more views of Lake Templene. Wildflowers often grow between the water and the road throughout much of the summer.

Beginning at *Mile 19.4* the road twists and curves and within a half mile you cycle by Glen Oaks Community College. (To lengthen this route, you can cycle through the campus and enjoy the view from the hill overlooking Lake Templene). At *Mile 20.7* turn right (north) on Shimmel Road, a paved avenue with gravel shoulders and more traffic than the rest of the route. Finish your day by turning left (west) on M-86 at *Mile 22*. ▲ *Caution: M-86 has heavy traffic.* You are now back in the Centreville and will reach the Village Market at *Mile 23.3*.

Shorter Option (15 miles) This entire route is on paved roads, making it ideal for road bicycles. Turn left out of the Village Market parking lot in Centreville onto M-86. Cycle three blocks to Clinton Road; turn right. Cycle one block to Market Street; turn right (east) and this road soon becomes Truckenmiller Road. Turn right (south) on Rambadt Road, a road that winds down by Lake Templene and becomes Findley Road. Turn right (south) on Nottawa Road (or turn left on Nottawa Road and cycle into the town of Nottawa for an ice cream break at the Sand Lake Party Store & Ice Cream). Turn right (west) on Sauger Lake Road (also County Road 147) and then right (north) on Shimmel Road (also County Road 138) to return to M-86 where you head left for the Village Market parking lot.

Bicycle sales, service

The Kickstand, Maple Lane Plaza, 1100 North Main St., Three Rivers; ☎ (616) 278-7305.

Cottin's Hardware, Sturgis Plaza, Sturgis; ☎ (616) 651-9286.

The Kickstand Schwinn Cyclery, 1303 East Chicago Rd., Sturgis; ☎ (616) 651-5088.

Village Cyclery, 148 N Grand, Schoolcraft; ☎ (616) 679-4242.

Area events and festivals

June: Three Rivers Water Festival, Three Rivers.

July: Covered Bridge Days, Centreville.

August: Colon Magic Festival, Colon.

September: St. Joseph County Grange Fair, Centreville; Fall Tour bikeathon, Sturgis.

October: Three Rivers Color Tour, Three Rivers.

Area attractions

Abbott's Magic Manufacturing Co., Colon; ☎ (616) 432-3235.

Travel information

River Country Tourism Council, Box 70, Centreville, MI 49032; ☎ (800) 447-2821, *www.rivercountry.com* (free 20-page booklet available on 12 bicycle routes in St. Joseph County).

St. Joseph County Parks & Recreation; ☎ (616) 467-6361.

Sturgis Chamber of Commerce; ☎ (616) 651-5758.

Three Rivers Area Chamber of Commerce; ☎ (616) 278-8193.

A cyclist pauses on one of the many rail-trails that have been developed in Michigan from abandoned railroads.

Kal-Haven Trail

Trip Card

Starting Point: Kalamazoo
Counties: Kalamazoo, Van Buren
Distance: 34 miles
Shorter option: 16.8 miles
Terrain: flat, converted rail bed
Highlights: Kalamazoo, covered bridges, Bloomingdale train depot, wildflowers, blueberries, South Haven
Suggested riders: beginners

Imagine a trail from one of Michigan's largest cities to one of its nicest resort towns. Imagine a relaxing journey past blueberry fields, wildflowers, through quaint villages...a tour that takes you over seven bridges. Imagine no more, it's the Kal-Haven Trail, a route where friendly folks greet you along the way, ask you how far you've come, and give suggestions on where to eat.

This woodsy trail makes you feel like a kid again on a grand adventure! At one point, west of Gobles, my friend and I were pleasantly refreshed by the peaceful aura of the route. At this exceptionally scenic spot along the 34-mile journey, you will find a babbling brook with wildflowers interspersed between rocks and water. This cycling adventure into the woods and country is easily accessible for many city dwellers, whether they live in Chicago, Kalamazoo, South Bend or Grand Rapids.

The Kal-Haven Trail State Park is an abandoned rail line linking Kalamazoo to South Haven. The route attracted railroad builders as early as 1836, a year before Michigan statehood, and when the railroads prospered in the 1870's, towns popped up. Today, these same towns now provide food and lodging for cyclists and other trail users who have replaced rail passengers. Because the rail was routed to avoid steep hills it makes 34-mile trail ideal for beginning mountain bikers.

Much of the trail is made of crushed screened cinder slag or crushed screened limestone, which is best for mountain or hybrid bicycles, although road bicycles are acceptable. I usually ride a 12-speed bicycle but used my mountain bike on the Kal-Haven Trail. Mountain bicycles allow you to lean more freely from side to side or sit upright for a better view of the natural surroundings. The Kal-Haven is best cycled at a leisurely pace so you can stop often to enjoy the scenery.

Trail Fees: This rail-trail approach to park management is similar to the Hart-Montague Trail in Oceana County. The trail was built as a state park and is now jointly operated by the Friends of the Kal-Haven Trail and the Michigan Department of Natural Resources. The Friends of the Kal-Haven Trail finance the operation and maintenance of the trail through user fees and private donations.

Annual or day passes are required and can be purchased at the east and west trailheads, the Van Buren State Park, at the depot caboose in Bloomingdale, from trail rangers or at any business displaying the trail logo. In South Haven, trail passes can be purchased at several locations, including Cousin's Restaurant and Campground on Blue Star Highway and the South Haven Chamber of Commerce on Quaker Street.

The romance of the railroad era comes alive in the town of Bloomingdale with its historic, refurbished train depot, and a caboose that serves as an information center. It is a great spot to begin or end your ride, if you don't want to pedal the whole trail. Bloomingdale has parking for vehicles as well as restaurants and shops. Approximately eight miles from Kalamazoo is Mentha, where nearby fields of dark and very moist soil were once the world's largest producer of peppermint and spearmint.

Then there is Kalamazoo, a pleasant city of 80,000 and home of Western Michigan University. Kalamazoo has a variety of attractions and activities to enjoy before or after your ride or for non-cyclists who agree to wait for you. There is an aviation history museum in Kalamazoo, a classic car museum in nearby Hickory Corners and the Celery Flats Interpretive Center, in Portage, that traces the history of when the area was renowned for its celery farms.

Stage One (9.9 miles) The east trailhead is near Kalamazoo, just west of US-131 and two miles north of M-43, on 10th Street in Oshtemo Township (follow the signs). The staging area includes parking for 150 vehicles, trail signs, a picnic area, toilets and a renovated caboose that serves as an information center and is staffed by volunteers during the summer.

In the beginning, the trail winds northward and across the first of seven bridges that were previously railroad trestles. The initial stretch is through a hilly area that is especially pretty in the spring when wildflowers are in full bloom. It's hard not to be impressed with the woods and natural surrounding of this leg of the route.

The next bridge is near Mentha, where the land changes to flat, open fields, and is followed by another bridge (an old cattle crossing) as you approach Kendall, located just north of the trail at *Mile 10.* In Kendall, you'll find restrooms and places for refreshments.

Stage Two (8.4 miles) Continue west from Kendall and at *Mile 13.4,* you arrive at Gobles, another small, unpretentious town. In Gobles, try an old-fashioned soda or malt at Gobles Pharmacy or a sandwich at the deli at the Gobles Grocery. The next town west of Gobles is Bloomingdale, reached at *Mile 18.3.* Bloomingdale, with its wonderfully restored depot, is a popular place to park your car to pedal only a portion of the trail as opposed to the entire 34 miles. For food, Bloomingdale has the 4-Way Stop Grocery with a deli, located just 300 feet east of the trail information center.

Stage Three (15.8 miles) From Bloomingdale, get back in the saddle, and - you guessed it - head west. You'll cycle over an intriguing old camelback bridge crossing Barber Creek and then past the towns of Grand Junction at *Mile 24.5* and Lacota at *Mile 27.4*. In both villages, there are several choices for food (do we ever stop eating? No!), including fresh sandwiches at the Country Cupboard in Grand Junction.

From Lacota, there are less than seven miles to the trail's end. Keep heading west. The largest trestle, now a scenic covered bridge, spans the Black River, near South Haven. Just beyond *Mile 34* you've reached your final destination; the resort community of South Haven, located on Lake Michigan. The South Haven trailhead is along the Black River . It is located on Bailey Street behind the courthouse, northeast of downtown South Haven. It's a quarter mile north of Phoenix Street, South Haven's main shopping and restaurant area. At the trailhead there's an asphalt parking lot and a couple of vault toilets. This trailhead was moved in 1998 from Blue Star Highway.

South Haven is home to the Michigan Maritime Museum, art galleries, gift shops, bed & breakfast establishments and, of course, inviting Lake Michigan beaches. Just south of town is the Van Buren State Park, a great place to set up camp or to enjoy a picnic.

Shorter Option (16.8 miles) From the train depot in Bloomingdale, head east on the trail, by the town of Gobles, and then by Kendall. Stop in Gobles or Kendall along the way, and then backtrack to Bloomingdale.

Bicycle sales, service

Alfred E. Bike, 320 E. Michigan Ave., Kalamazoo; ☎ (616) 349-9423.

Billy's Bike Shop, 63 E. Battlecreek St., Galesburg; ☎ (616) 665-5202.

Breakaway Bicycles, 185 Romence Rd., Portage; ☎ (616) 324-5555.

Millwood Schwinn, 1015 E. Cork Rd., Kalamazoo; ☎ (616) 349-6384.

Parchment Bicycle, 5348 Riverview, Parchment; ☎ (616) 343-8118.

Portage Schwinn Cyclery, 300 E. Centre, Portage; ☎ (616) 327-3393.

Riverview Equipment & Bait, 53804 County Road-687, Hartford; ☎ (616) 621-4791.

Vornkamp Bike, 673 Lake, Kalamazoo; ☎ (616) 344-3599.

Area events and festivals

April: Kitefest, Kalamazoo.

May: Kal-Haven Trail Blazer; Mayfair, Kalamazoo.

June: Celery Flats Arts & Craft Fair, Portage.

July: National Blueberry Festival, South Haven; Flowerfest, Kalamazoo.

September: Celery Fest, Portage; Michigan Wine & Harvest Festival, Paw Paw.

Area attractions

Gilmore Car Museum, Hickory Corners; ☎ (616) 671-5089, *www.gilmorecarmuseum.org*.

Kalamazoo Aviation Museum, Kalamazoo; ☎ (616) 382-6555.

Celery Flats Interpretive Center, Portage; ☎ (616) 329-4522.

Kalamazoo Public Museum; ☎ (616) 345-7092.

Kalamazoo Nature Center; ☎ (616)381-1574.

St. Julian Winery, Paw Paw; ☎ (616) 657-5568, *www.stjulian.com*.

Warner Vineyards, Paw Paw; ☎ (616) 657-3165.

Michigan Maritime Museum, South Haven; ☎ (616) 637-8078.

Travel information

Kal-Haven Trail; ☎ (616) 637-2788 or (616) 637-4984.

Kalamazoo Convention & Visitors Bureau; ☎ (616) 381-4003 or (800) 222-6363, *www.kzoobiz.com*.

Paw Paw Chamber of Commerce; ☎ (616) 657-5395.

Lakeshore Visitors Bureau, South Haven; ☎ (616) 637-5252 or (800) 764-2836, *www.southhavenmi.com*.

South Haven Chamber of Commerce; ☎ (616) 637-5171.

7 Battle Creek Linear Park

Trip Card

Starting point: Western trailhead on Dickman Road
Distance: 17.5 miles
Shorter option: 10.3 miles
Terrain: flat, a few rolling hills
Highlights: Cereal City, Underground Railroad Sculpture, Kalamazoo River
Suggested riders: beginners

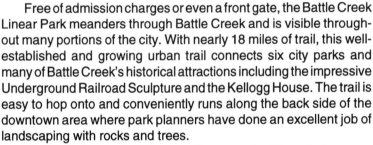

Free of admission charges or even a front gate, the Battle Creek Linear Park meanders through Battle Creek and is visible throughout many portions of the city. With nearly 18 miles of trail, this well-established and growing urban trail connects six city parks and many of Battle Creek's historical attractions including the impressive Underground Railroad Sculpture and the Kellogg House. The trail is easy to hop onto and conveniently runs along the back side of the downtown area where park planners have done an excellent job of landscaping with rocks and trees.

The trail stays primarily away from roads although there are some busy streets to cross. At times you'll follow wooden bridges that dip under overpasses with brightly colored murals. Many parts of the trail follow the Kalamazoo and Battle Creek rivers. It's a unique trail with 50 educational signs featuring plant, animal, historical and cultural points of interest.

When traveling from the western trailhead and approaching the downtown area, riders can't help but be drawn to Cereal City U.S.A., a new tourist attraction established by the Kellogg Corporation in 1998. The town of Battle Creek is synonymous with cereal and the large Cereal City is a tribute to the company's long tradition. Kids will enjoy seeing how cereal is boxed on simulated working production line and the interactive exhibits. The large gift shop includes an impressive collection of Kellogg memorabilia from Tony the Tiger cups and Rice Krispies characters to old cereal advertisements.

BATTLE CREEK LINEAR PARK

The trail gives a good overview of what Battle Creek has to offer, showing off schools, a college campus, gardens and woods. The most notable restaurant near the trail is Clara's, located in a refurbished train depot between Capital Avenue and McCamly Avenue on the north side of the river. Also in the downtown area is Schlotzsky's Deli on State Street for sandwiches and personal pizzas.

Stage One (6.6 miles) To reach the western trailhead from I-94 depart at exit 95 and head north on Helmer Road and then west on Dickman Road. The trailhead is on Dickman just east of where it splits with Business I-94. Park anywhere in this industrial park area. Although there are no restrooms or other amenities at this trailhead, rest assured there are plenty of businesses with restrooms and picnic areas along the way.

The trail heads east towards downtown Battle Creek. In less than a mile you cross West River Road and reach a scenic wooded section along the Kalamazoo River. Helmer Road is reached at *Mile 3* and a half mile beyond it is another staging area near the Kalamazoo River at the corner of Jackson Street and 20th Street. From 20th Street you'll make the swift journey into downtown Battle Creek. At *Mile 6.6* you'll pass the colorful Cereal City where you can take a breather outside on bench. To your right is the downtown area with many eating and shopping options. That includes a shopping area called McCamly Place, a block and a half south of the trail on the corner of McCamly Avenue and Jackson Street.

Stage Two (5 miles) Just past Cereal City lies a string of attractions as well as numerous spots to pick up the trail. Team Active Cycling & Fitness, one of the largest bike shops in Michigan, is in downtown area and features a colorful mural on the back side of their building. Also nearby is Friendship Park, a small scenic park

Bailey Park

Wagner Dr.

East Ave.

9.6 miles

Battle Creek River

Union St.

Roosevelt Ave.

Kalamazoo Community College

Emmett St.

Capital Ave.

11.6 miles

North St.

Division St.

Goodale Ave

Washington St.

6.6 miles

Cereal City

Kendall St.

Hubbard St.

Kalamazoo River

13.5 miles

Limit St.

Leila Arboretum

West Michigan Ave.

20th St.

3.6 miles

Battle Creek Linear Park

Jackson St.

Helmer Rd.

West River Rd.

Start 0.0
Finish 17.5 miles

Dickman Rd.

61

A cyclist pauses on the Battle Creek Linear Park trail at Kellogg' Corporation's Cereal City USA.

along the trail.

Continuing east you'll cruise by the historic Kellogg House and the Underground Railroad Sculpture, a large monument dedicated to Battle Creek's role as an important stop for slaves seeking their freedom in the 1800s. The trail then crosses the Kalamazoo River and reaches a wooden boardwalk along the river at *Mile 9.* You continue along the river to pass Verona Dam overlook and then cross Wagner Drive to enter Bailey Park. There are restrooms in this large park. **A** *Caution: when leaving Bailey Park be alert at Capital Avenue, by far the busiest road you will cross during the ride.*

Nearby are fast food options such as Kentucky Fried Chicken and Taco Bell. Before you reach the grounds of Kellogg Community College at *Mile 11.6* you pass through some residential sections and enjoy a fun two-stage downhill stretch. A spur of the Battle Creek Linear Park encircles Kellogg Community College, a small college with a pleasant campus.

Stage Three (5.9 miles) To continue along the perimeter of the trail stay to the right where you cross Roosevelt Street and encounter a sizable climb. This section of the trail, from the college to Dudley Elementary School, is not as scenic as other segments but your efforts are rewarded later when you reach the Leila Arboretum at *Mile 13.5.* At the arboretum you can briefly depart the Battle Creek Linear Park and follow a one-mile path through the 72 acres of landscaped gardens.

Leila Arboretum is at West Michigan Avenue at 20th Street and includes seasonal floral displays, children's adventure gardens, a sunken garden and a visitor center. Also located within the park is the Kingman Museum of Natural History with three floors of exhibits covering everything from dinosaurs to stars in the universe. Both the gardens and the museum make a nice place for an extended break. Continue southwest on Battle Creek Linear Park trail and within a short distance you'll reach the corner of Jackson Street and 20th Street. To return to the Dickman Road trailhead, cross Jackson Street and backtrack the first leg of the outing. The trailhead will be reached at *Mile 17.5.*

Shorter Option (10.3 miles) Following the perimeter of the trail from the corner of 20th Street and Jackson Street is a 10.3-mile ride. You find a trailhead and parking area west of the intersection on Jackson Street. Many other shorter options are possible from trailheads in the downtown area. One spur of the Battle Creek Linear Park also connects the downtown area with Kellogg Community College to the north.

Bicycle sales, service

Team Active Cycling & Fitness, 22 W. Michigan Ave., Battle Creek; ☎ (616) 962-7688.

Getaway Sports, 2809 Capital Ave. SW, Battle Creek; ☎ (616) 979-1996.

Area events and festivals

June: World's Largest Breakfast Table, Cereal Festival Parade, Battle Creek

July: Hot Air Balloon Championships, Taste of Battle Creek; Battle Creek

Area attractions

Binder Park Zoo, Battle Creek; ☎ (616) 979-1351.

Kellogg's Cereal City USA, Battle Creek; ☎ (616) 962-6230.

Full Blast Entertainment Center, Battle Creek; ☎ (616) 966-3667.

Cornwell's Turkeyville USA, Marshall; ☎ (616) 781-4293 or (800) 228-4315.

Leila Arboretum and Kingman Museum, Battle Creek: ☎ (616) 969-0270.

Travel information

Battle Creek Parks and Recreation Department; ☎ (616) 966-3431.

Battle Creek/Calhoun County Visitors Bureau; ☎ (616) 962-2240 or (800) 397-2240; *www.battlecreek.org.*

Saugatuck Tour

Trip Card

Starting point: Saugatuck
County: Allegan
Distance: 36 miles
Shorter option: 7 to 10 miles
Terrain: mostly flat
Highlights: Kalamazoo River,
Saugatuck, Mount Baldhead Park,
Chain Ferry, Fennville, Hutchins Lake
Suggested riders: beginners to intermediate

Tucked away off of I-196 on the Kalamazoo River near Lake Michigan is the town of Saugatuck. Trendy boutiques, art galleries and restaurants accessible by boat as well as cars are all a part of busy Saugatuck. Maybe it's the ambience, but visitors to this resort town always seem relaxed and happy. As the bed & breakfast capital of Michigan, Saugatuck boasts more than 15 of these establishments, from Victorian homes to country settings. Moored at the edge of its downtown shopping district is an impressive armada of cabin cruisers, yachts and bobbing sailboats.

The shorter loop of this circuit, 7.2 to 10.4 miles, has to be one of the most scenic in West Michigan and, in this honeymooner's haunt of a town, can even be called romantic. The route starts in Saugatuck, leads you through shaded woods and spectacular Lake Michigan scenery, and ends with a wonderful opportunity to travel across the Kalamazoo River on a chain-powered ferry.

The start of both loops is at Wicks Park on Water Street, where public restrooms feature an impressionist painting on the side (only in Saugatuck!). This is a great place to lock up your bicycles after your ride to go people watching, boat watching (it's debatable which is more intriguing in Saugatuck) or enjoy the town's wide variety of restaurants. Stroll along Butler or Water streets, buy some fudge or that "gotta have it" Saugatuck T-shirt.

The longer 36.7-mile loop winds its way out of Saugatuck to just south of the Holland area, then through open countryside to Fennville. Although Fennville is only five miles away from Saugatuck, the two towns are in direct contrast to each other. Sleepy little Fennville is best known for its October Goose Festival. The nearby Allegan State Game area and the Todd Farm attract flocks of Canada geese in the fall and thus goose watchers. During the two-day festival there's a goose calling championship, a goose arts and crafts show, a 10-kilometer Wild Goose Chase, and a parade. Or any time of the year you can stop at the Blue Goose Cafe (☎ 616-561-5044) for its roasted chicken, a Friday night fish fry or a Blue Goose omelette. The Blue Goose Cafe is an ideal stop halfway through the longer route for a light meal or snack.

Whether you undertake the long or short option, the addition of boat cruises, a chain ferry, dune rides, and a steamship tour with pleasant cycling, food and shopping, add up to a day or two, or even three days, of fun in Allegan County.

Stage One (14.7 miles) Head north on Water Street and then turn right on Lucy Street, left on Holland, and then another left on Blue Star Highway at *Mile 1.4*. Travel for a mile on Blue Star Highway, which can be busy, and just before the I-196 overpass, turn left on 64th Street, where Saugatuck State Park is signposted. Heading north you actually pass within a mile of the entrance to the state park. The undeveloped unit features hiking trails, scenic dunes and uncrowded beaches because it's a mile walk from the parking lot to Lake Michigan.

At *Mile 7.6*, turn right on 146th Street and head east through the tiny village of Graafschap reached at *Mile 9.3*. Turn right (south) on 60th Street, enter rolling open country and tackle an uphill segment at *Mile 10.8*. Turn left (east) on 136th Avenue at *Mile 14.7* to complete the first stage.

Stage Two (7.8 miles) Cycle less than a mile on 136th Avenue to 58th Street and turn right. There's a picturesque Christmas tree farm on your right at *Mile 18* and horse stables on your left at *Mile 21.3*. From the stables you'll soon see the "Welcome to Fennville" sign and then turn left (east) onto 124th Street (also labeled M-89), the main road into downtown Fennville. Time for a break, a stroll

through the small town or possibly lunch at the Blue Goose Cafe reached at *Mile 22.5* into the tour. Breakfast is served anytime, so you can load up on carbohydrates with the cafe's Belgian waffle.

Stage Three (13.4 miles) Head west out of Fennville on 124th Street (M-89) back to 58th Avenue and turn left (south) this time. Within two miles this road curves west around Hutchins Lake and becomes 122nd Avenue as you skirt the shoreline. Turn right (north) onto 62nd Street which leads past Fenn Valley Vineyards (☎ 616-561-2396). At the winery visitors can enjoy a self-guided tour of vineyard and cellar operations, watch an audiovisual program on "wine appreciation" and do a little wine tasting. Just remember you still have another 10 miles left of the tour. Don't get too mellow.

Continue north on 62nd Street, cross 124th Street to Riverside Drive, which veers to the left at *Mile 30.6*. Although there is little shoulder along Riverside, this is still a pleasant road for cycling as it curves and winds its way back to Douglas. Eventually Riverside turns into 130th Avenue and you're back in Douglas at *Mile 32.5*. Turn right (north) on Blue Star Highway (⚠ *Caution: busy*) at *Mile 33.7* and then left on Lake Street at *Mile 35*. From here it's back to Wicks Park and the starting point. Food time (of course!) or simply enjoy the colorful, casual atmosphere of this placid resort community.

Shorter Option (7.2 - 10.4 miles) Begin at Wicks Park, on Water Street near the public restrooms and turn right on Lucy Street and then immediately right on Butler Street. Walk bicycles in this main shopping area to avoid a collision (and to see what stores you want to stop at later!). Take a left on Culver Street at *Mile 0.6*, which turns into Lake Street, pedal uphill and then turn right onto Blue Star Highway at *Mile 1.3* to cross the Kalamazoo River. To the west is Harbor Village where you'll find *SS Keewatin* Ship Tours, City of Douglas Dinner Cruises and a store to stock up on food and drink.

Turn right (west) on Center Street at *Mile 2* and head west past two bed and breakfast establishments within a mile. Kirby House, built in 1890, appears first and is followed by the Sherwood Forest Bed and Breakfast, both on the right side of Center Street. At *Mile 3*, turn left on Lake Shore Drive. This road is narrow but shady as it skirts the edge of a bluff overlooking Lake Michigan. Head south to the Lake Shore Resort (☎ 616-857-7121), where there is a great vantage point to enjoy the Lake Michigan shoreline and dunes in the

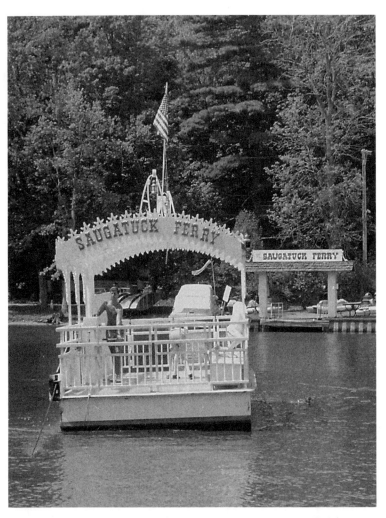

The historic Saugatuck Chain Ferry crosses the Kalamazoo River in downtown Saugatuck.

distance.

    From the lookout point at Lake Shore Resort, backtrack on Lake Shore Drive. Rosemont Inn, an elegant bed and breakfast, is reached at *Mile 5.5* and a half mile beyond it you turn right on Shorewood Drive, which turns into Campbell Road. Turn left on Park

❀❀❀❀❀❀❀❀❀❀❀❀❀❀❀❀❀❀❀❀❀

The Saugatuck Chain Ferry

The most unusual vessel afloat in Saugatuck or perhaps anywhere along Lake Michigan is the Saugatuck Chain Ferry. It's the only chain-powered ferry in the state and a 160-year tradition in Saugatuck. When the original one, a chain-pulled wooden barge, was put into service in 1838, it was a much heralded event. Before then, friends and farmers spent a half day traveling 10 miles inland to a bridge in New Richmond, just to reach Douglas, which was only 100 yards across the river.

The tradition stayed alive even after the Saugatuck-Douglas bridge was completed in the 1920s. In 1965, The Peterson Co. built the present ferry, a small barge with white gingerbread siding and a 380-foot chain to pull it through the water. The chain ferry operates daily from the second weekend in June through Labor Day, and the trip lasts a mere 15 to 20 minutes, delivering passengers just south of Mount Baldhead Park.

❀❀❀❀❀❀❀❀❀❀❀❀❀❀❀❀❀❀❀❀❀

Street at *Mile 6.4* and you're back in the Saugatuck city limits.

At *Mile 7.2* you've arrived at Mount Baldhead Park, where there are restrooms, a shelter and picnic tables. There is also a stairway that leads to the top of the 200-foot dune where you'll find observation decks and a fantastic view of Saugatuck, the Kalamazoo River and Lake Michigan. Trails on the other side lead down to Oval Beach, where MTV once filmed a segment.

Back at the park you have the option of taking the Saugatuck Chain Ferry across the river back to the starting point. It's a small fee for a ride on the only hand-powered ferry in the state. Or you can save a buck or two by pedaling around the river back to the starting point, via Park Street and then left on Center Street at *Mile 8.5*. Within a third of a mile turn left on Blue Star Highway. ⚠ *Caution: Blue Star Highway can be very busy*. Finally turn left on Lake Street at *Mile 9.5*, which curves to the right into Water Street within a half mile. At *Mile 10.4*, you're back at Wicks Park.

Bicycle sales, service

Cross Country Cycle, 137 N. River Ave., Holland; ☎ (616) 396-7491.

Holland Schwinn Cyclery, 326 South River Avenue; Holland; ☎ (616) 393-0046.

Area events and festivals

July: Harbor Days/Venetian Festival, Saugatuck.

August: Arts and crafts shows, Saugatuck.

September: Jazz Festival, Saugatuck/Douglas.

October: Halloween Harvest Festival, Saugatuck; Goose Festival, Fennville.

Area attractions

"M/V City of Douglas" (scenic and dinner cruises); ☎ (616) 857-2151, ext. 26, or (616) 857-2107.

Saugatuck Boat Cruises; ☎ (616) 857-4261.

Saugatuck Chain Ferry; ☎ (616) 857-2151, ext. 26, or (616) 857-2107

"SS Keewatin" (Maritime Museum on a Great Lakes steamship); ☎ (616) 857-2107.

Fenn Valley Winery, Fennville; ☎ (800) 432-6265.

Travel information

Saugatuck/Douglas Convention and Visitors Bureau; ☎ (616) 857-1701, *www.saugatuck.com*.

Fennville Area Chamber of Commerce; ☎ (616) 561-5550.

Holland Area Chamber of Commerce; ☎ (616) 392-2389, www.hollandchamber.org.

Holland Convention & Visitors Bureau; ☎ (800) 506-1299.

Dutch Delight

Trip Card

Starting point: Holland
County: Ottawa
Distance: 51 miles
Shorter option: 20 miles
Terrain: relatively flat, some rolling hills
Highlights: Tunnel Park, Lake Michigan, Dutch attractions, Grand Haven, Holland State Park
Suggested riders: beginners for shorter option, intermediate for longer loop

Riding three abreast on bike trails that follow Lake Michigan and weave in and around a pleasant community- that's the joy of a 51-mile (and 20-mile shorter option) bicycle loop from Holland to Grand Haven. Holland's widespread reputation of a tourist town full of tulips and Dutch attractions has made this area bicycle-friendly for all ages, from a child following Lake Michigan for a mile or so to competitive cyclists looking for a 51-mile training loop.

There are many miles of bike paths in Ottawa County that are separate from roads, yet follow them. One of the highlights of this route is the bike path on Lake Shore Avenue which traverses rolling hills through canopies of trees in full, lush foliage while skirting Lake Michigan. Experienced cyclists can ride this path from Tunnel Park, near Holland State Park, all the way to another delightful tourist town, Grand Haven.

Families whose members have different cycling abilities will also enjoy the area. In the summer, spouse and kids can travel as far as they want to and then backtrack to Holland State Park on Lake Michigan. While waiting for the more experienced cyclist to finish the longer loop, they can enjoy one of the finest beaches in the state as well as "Big Red," Holland's landmark lighthouse, and numerous eateries nearby.

The longer, 51-mile loop travels for three miles on James Street, a road that gives you an idea of the Dutch heritage of this town. On the corner of US-31 and James Street is Manufacturers Marketplace with more than 55 brand name outlet stores. It's a true shopper's delight whether you're looking for dish towels to match your Pfaltzgraff dinnerware, sweatpants for the whole family or rock bottom prices on toys.

Near the mall there's also the Country Inn by Carlson (☎ 616-396-6677) with its Dutch facade for convenient lodging. At Dutch Village, on the same corner, you can watch wooden shoes being made or shop for handcrafted items. What about food? If you're looking for more than hot dogs-on-the-beach, there are several fine dining establishments in Holland such as the Hatch, 1870 Ottawa Beach Rd. Better than fast food, but just as cheap, are the three Russ' Restaurants in Holland (☎ 616-396-2348), serving West Michigan style meals - lots of food for a moderate price. Near the Holland State Park, there's the Ottawa Beach Inn Restaurant, 2155 Ottawa Beach Rd., perfect for tired, happy cyclists.

Stage One (10.9 miles) From Tunnel Park on Lake Shore Avenue just north of Holland State Park, head north on the bike path. You'll have to cross a couple of roads and travel partially on the shoulder where it's necessary to watch out for private driveways. But for the most part it's clear sailing to your first stop, Kirk Park, south of Grand Haven. Early in this circuit, you'll find many segments shaded by a canopy of trees, including a half-mile stretch at *Mile 1.5*. Unlike the mostly flat rail trails, this bike path features a number of rolling but fun hills that also attract walkers, joggers, in-line skaters and other non-motorized users.

At *Mile 4.8* you pedal through a series of forested rolling hills where in the spring a variety of wildflowers can be spotted along the edge. A bridge spanning the Pigeon River is crossed at *Mile 7.5* followed by a stretch through open country where the trail is occasionally the shoulder of the road. At *Mile 8.6* you're back on the bike paths and the last mile before your first stop, Kirk Park, is another delightful ride through a hardwood forest. Ottawa County's Kirk Park is reached at *Mile 10.7* and is a good place for an extended break to cool off your feet with a wade in the "big lake." There are

restrooms located in the park.

Stage Two (8.4 miles) From Kirk Park, head north on the bike path through another stand of pine before Hiawatha Drive and then across a wooden plank section of the trail near *Mile 12.* The bike path continues along Lake Shore Avenue and is often hidden from the road, as it diverts into the forest offering a pleasant route. There's a cemetery on the right at *Mile 14.8* and just beyond *Mile 18* you pass the "Welcome to Grand Haven" sign.

Grand Haven is home of the Musical Fountain, another classic lighthouse and one of the most colorful river walks in the state. Here you'll travel on sidewalks to Washington Street in the heart of the city reached at *Mile 19.3.* Time to stop at a restaurant, take a water break or a side jaunt to Grand Haven State Park that can be reached by following the boardwalk along the Grand River. You'll also find a Russ' Restaurant in Grand Haven at 1313 S. Beacon Blvd.

Stage Three (11.7 miles) Turn right on Washington Street in Grand Haven. You'll be traveling on wide sidewalks. ⚠ *Be careful at the busy intersection here, especially Beacon Boulevard, both are very busy.* Turn right (south) on Beechtree at Mile 20.8 where you'll pass through an industrial section before taking a left on Robbins Road at *Mile 21.5.*

At *Mile 22.2* you return to bike trails (eeeha!). Pass 160th Avenue and turn right (south) onto Mercury Drive at *Mile 22.8* to begin a long, level stretch of bike path that's interrupted briefly by a short segment of gravel shoulder. A bayou off the Grand River is crossed near *Mile 25.* Turn right (south) onto 144th Avenue and then left (east) onto Lincoln Avenue. Refreshment break! At the corner of Lincoln and 128th Avenue is Spinner's Grocery Store for a good dose of junk food. There are no bike paths on Lincoln Street, but the road has fairly light traffic and is a level route through pleasant farm country.

Stage Four (12.8 miles) Turn right at the corner of Lincoln Avenue and 120th Avenue and head south on 120th Avenue for more than 10 miles. This stretch is a flat and straight ride through more farmland and Christmas tree farms. This road is an excellent choice when the weather is cooler, allowing you to avoid the sometimes chilly lake breezes. On 120th Avenue you'll pass the Pigeon Creek County Park at *Mile 34.6* and the South Olive Christian Reformed Church at *Mile 38.4.* As can clearly be seen from

The riverwalk and lighthouse in Grand Haven.

this road, the Holland area is a stronghold for the Christian Reformed Church which was formed here in 1857. It's been estimated that a third of the denomination's members live in West Michigan.

At *Mile 43.3* is the intersection of James Street and 120th Avenue, the end of the fourth stage. Time to get off the bike, stretch your legs and prepare for the short and final leg back to Tunnel Park.

Stage Five (7.6 miles) Turn right (west) on James Street and soon you'll be back on the bike trails. Travel to corner of James Street and US-31 where you'll find a Wendy's along with Manufacturer's Marketplace, Westshore Mall and Dutch Village - all pre and post ride options. You've ridden 43.8 miles when you reach this bustling shopping area. ⚠ *Caution: US-31 is a very busy highway to cross.* Continue west on James Street and cross Butternut Drive. Turn left on Division (144th Avenue) where you'll still be on the narrow bike trail.

Near *Mile 47* turn right on Lakewood Boulevard. Go up a slight hill, cross 152nd Avenue and then prepare for more rolllling, rolllllling hills; a fun stretch for everybody! Now it's back to Lake Shore Avenue where you turn left to get back to the starting point at Tunnel Park. Or else stay on the trail for 1.6 miles to reach Lake Macatawa. From here you can turn right (west) on 168th to continue to Holland

Holland Harbor Lighthouse across from Holland State Park

State Park for a stroll on the beach or to take in the catamarans, sailboats and other boats entering Lake Michigan. Food??? The Ottawa Beach Inn Restaurant is located near the entrance of the state park.

Shorter option (20 miles) Head north out of Tunnel Park on the bike paths and pass Quincy, Ransom, New Holland and Van Buren streets. Turn right on Wildwood (which veers northeast) and then turn right (south) on Butternut Drive, which also has bike paths. Cycle south on Butternut Drive to 144th Avenue where you turn right (west) onto Lakewood Boulevard. Lakewood Boulevard deadends at Lake Shore Avenue where you can head south on the bike path to return to Tunnel Park.

Bicycle sales, service

Cross Country Cycle, 137 N. River Ave., Holland; ☎ (616) 396-7491.

Holland Schwinn Cyclery, 326 South River Avenue, Holland; ☎ (616) 393-0046.

Bikeaway Bicycles, 215 N. Ferry St., Grand Haven; ☎(616) 844-1199.

Rock 'n' Road Cycle, 300 N. Seventh St., Grand Haven; ☎(616) 846-2800.

Zeeland Schwinn Cyclery, 201 E. Main Ave., Zeeland; ☎(616) 772-6223.

Area events and festivals

May: Tulip Time Festival, Holland.

June: Libertyfest, Holland; Sand Sculpture Contest, Grand Haven.

July: Classic Boat Rendezvous, Grand Haven; Up in Central Park Art Show, Grand Haven.

August: Coast Guard Festival, Grand Haven

October: Fall Color Fest, Grand Haven.

Area attractions

Dutch Village; ☎ (616) 396-1475.

Veldheer Tulip Gardens, DeKlomp Wooden Shoe & Delftware Factory; ☎ (616) 399-1900.

Windmill Island; ☎ (616) 355-1035, *www.windmillisland.org*.

Musical Fountain, Grand Haven; ☎ (616) 842-4499.

Travel information

Holland Area Convention & Visitors Bureau, ☎ (616) 394-0000 or (800) 506-1299, *www.holland.org*.

Holland Chamber of Commerce; ☎ (616) 392-2389, *www.hollandchamber.org*.

Grand Haven/Spring Lake Visitors Bureau, ☎ (616) 842-4499 or (800) 303-4088, *www.grandhavenchamber.org*.

Cyclists on Kent Trails cross the Grand River on a former railroad bridge.

10 Kent Trails

Trip Card

Starting point: Grand Rapids
County: Kent
Distance: 30 miles round trip
Shorter option: 7 to 10 miles
Terrain: flat, converted rail bed, some roads
Highlights: John Ball Park & Zoo, Johnson Park, Douglas Walker Park
Suggested riders: beginners

Cyclers! You may
be fantasizing
Tour D'France.

Wake up, It's
Kent County and this
is Tour D'Fence.

Enjoy your day
and when you
recall this ride,

Definitely plan
to Tour D'Sewer
side.

Wyoming invites
you to get off
your bicycle

Call (616) 534-8606
and learn how
to recycle.

This humorous poem greets cyclists heading north on the Kent Trails, a 15-mile trail dedicated in May 1992. So what's the charm of a trail partially fenced-in with (yech!) barbed wire, that travels over a new pipeline, and has a repaved road and an old rail trail? It's the fact that you're in Michigan's second largest metropolitan area and that you don't have to worry much about the pitfalls of automobile traffic.

The dream of this trail began in 1986 when the Penn Central

Railroad, interested in selling off its old rail line, contacted the Kent County Parks Department. With the help of a Michigan Department of Natural Resources grant, Kent County brought together six governmental bodies (not a small feat!) to make this vision of a single trail connecting three major parks in the Grand Rapids area a reality.

The trail begins in an urban setting, near a Coca Cola bottling plant, just south of the John Ball Park & Zoo. One nippy Sunday afternoon very early in the cycling season, we ventured onto the path and weren't immediately impressed with the high fences and small patches of barbed wire. But eventually the fence gave way to a winding pathway along the Grand River. We crossed a refurbished bridge, with new aqua-colored paint and fresh cement, yet we still knew it was a railroad bridge.

And at 1.7 miles into the trip the trail turned to Indian Mounds Road, where between 200 B.C. and 400 A.D. the Hopewellian Indian people created the mounds on the west bank of the Grand River, Michigan's longest river. Throughout the Kent Trails, the aqua-colored posts featuring the trail logo will keep you on track for the whole route.

After journeying 5.4 miles south to the trailhead at Prairie Street in Grandville, the ride turns into what a lot of touring cyclists love - a long, fast, flat, asphalt trail with no more than five percent grade. This segment winds through farmlands, new residential construction, past a golf course and under a bridge. The trail ends at the big white chicken of the Byron Center Hotel, whose sign reads "BAR-chicken dinners every Saturday night." From there it's 2.7 rolling miles on 84th Street to the final destination - Douglas Walker Park. We turned left on 84th Street in Byron Center, locked the bicycles and enjoyed a leisurely lunch of burgers and sandwiches at the Byron Family Restaurant (☎616-878-1888). This place has a great small-town appeal. After lunch, it was back on the trail for the return trip to John Ball Park & Zoo.

Grand Rapids is a bustling community known for its downtown fireworks on the Fourth of July, its Celebration on the Grand (an annual event which began when hometown boy Gerald R. Ford was president) in September and probably the largest, all-volunteer, local arts festival in the world held in June. The festival has been nicknamed "Foodfest" with delicacies such as souvlaki (Greek), elephant ears with cinnamon sugar, kielbasa (Polish) and, new in

Lake Michigan Dr.

GRAND RAPIDS

O'Brien St.

Wilson Rd.

JOHN BALL PARK

Start • 0 Miles

Finish • 30 Miles (round trip)

Short loop • 7 Miles

JOHNSON PARK

Burton St.

Ivanrest Ave.

28 th St.

Prairie St.

36 th St.

196

44 th St.

52 nd St.

Division St.

Wilson Rd.

Burlington

131

64 th St.

N

76 th St.

DOUGLAS WALKER PARK

BYRON CENTER

84 th St.

Cycling West Michigan

1992, Pavlovas (Australian whipped cream and fresh fruit, topped with meringue) and barbecue turkey drumsticks.

If you decide to do 30 miles round trip, your non-cycling friends and family members can ride a shorter loop and enjoy the zoo, eat their hearts out at a festival or in one of the area's hundreds of restaurants, or do some power shopping on 28th Street, Plainfield Avenue or Alpine Avenue (major shoppers' rows). That way everyone's happy, from Mom on down to the baby sister.

The trail is ideal for shorter loops, too. We recommend the 10.2 mile stretch from 44th Street to 84th Street (round trip), or the 7-mile trip (round trip) from the John Ball Park & Zoo to Johnson Park and back.

Stage One (5.4 miles) From John Ball Park & Zoo, head south on the trail near the Coca Cola bottling plant. This is an off-road section over a new pipeline. At *Mile 1.7* turn left and cross the Grand River on an old, but refurbished railroad bridge. Continue south on Indian Mounds Drive for 1.3 miles and then look for the Kent Trails posts that direct you to a short off-road section to Ivanrest Avenue.

Another option, instead of crossing the railroad bridge, is to keep riding on the off-road section over new pipeline and then onto Veterans Memorial Drive to Johnson Park. The 245-acre park is on the Grand River and features picnic facilities, fishing, trails and a playground.

At *Mile 3.6* you have the unique experience of traveling on a road with a wastewater plant on your left while on the other side is the West Michigan Readi Mix plant and West Michigan Recycled Aggregate. Talk about natural surroundings. Shortly after that, you arrive at an odd intersection on Ivanrest Avenue with a sharply-angled Chicago Drive. Continue on Ivanrest Avenue. ⚠ *Caution: This road can have heavy traffic depending on the time of day.* Cross 28th Street (busy, busy!) at *Mile 4.2* to Prairie Street. Take a left on Prairie Street and cycle less than a mile to the beginning of the rail trail. Whew! You made it.

Stage Two (5.3 miles) The trail is relaxing and, more important, flat, making enjoyable conversations possible. Cross 36th Street near *Mile 6* and look for the wooden bridge at *Mile 6.3*. In a half mile, take a left at Spartan Industrial Drive and follow the aqua-colored posts to the trailhead at 44th Street, which along with 36th Street, can be a busy road. But don't despair, from here on the trailhead is

The West Michigan Tourist Association

The West Michigan Tourist Association (WMTA) has been promoting the beauty and hospitality of this region of the state since the days of steamships on the Great Lakes and travel by trains. Founded in 1917, the association is the oldest continuously operating regional tourist association in the nation. For years WMTA was the only organization promoting Michigan and its annual publication *Carefree Days* (now the *West Michigan Travel Guide*) became an indispensable guide for information on where to stay, what to see and how to recreate in West Michigan.

Today WMTA publishes a variety of travel guides and brochures that assist tourists in their vacation plans. You request materials by visiting the WTMA website at *www.wmta.org* pass or calling the association at ☎ (800) 442-2084. If passing through Grand Rapids stop at the WTMA Visitor Center and gift shop at 1253 Front St. N.W., reached from US-131 by departing at exit 87 and heading west on Leonard Street.

a straight line to Byron Center. At *Mile 8.2*, you'll cross 52nd Street and at *Mile 10.7* you'll cross 72nd Street.

Stage Three (4.3 miles) For the final leg of the Kent Trails, travel 1.6 miles until the end of the rail trail at 84th Street; turn left. This road heads east 2.7 miles over rolling, long hills through downtown Byron Center to Douglas Walker Park. Byron Center is quintessential small-town America with several family restaurants and lots of chances for refreshing ice cream breaks. Another option is to leave the trail and turn left on 76th Street and then travel east for approximately 3 miles. Here 76th Street connects with another off-road bike path that leads south to Douglas Walker Park.

Bicycle sales, service
Alger Schwinn Cycling & Fitness, 120 28th St. SW, Grand Rapids; ☎ (616) 243-9753.

Alpine Cyclery, 3150 Alpine Ave. NW, Walker; ☎ (616) 785-0505.

Chicago Drive Schwinn Cycling & Fitness, 4300 Chicago Dr. SW, Grandville; ☎ (616) 531-9911

Freewheeler Bike Shop, 915 Leonard St. NW, Grand Rapids; ☎ (616) 451-8011.

Kentwood Schwinn Cycling & Fitness, 2830 East Paris SE, Kentwood; ☎ (616) 942-1880.

North Kent Schwinn, 4336 Plainfield Ave. NE; Grand Rapids; ☎ (616) 363-0705.

Village Bike Shop, 450 Baldwin St., Jenison; ☎ (616) 457-1670.

Village Bike Shop, 4252 Kalamazoo Ave. SE, Grand Rapids; ☎ (616) 455-4870.

Village Bike Shop, 2844 Thornapple River Dr. SE, Grand Rapids; ☎ (616) 285-1670.

Area events and festivals
May: Old Kent River Bank Run, Grand Rapids.
June: Festival of the Arts, Grand Rapids.
September: Celebration on the Grand, Grand Rapids.
October: Pulaski Days, Grand Rapids.

Area attractions
Blandford Nature Center, Grand Rapids; ☎ (616) 453-6192.
Van Andel Museum Center, Grand Rapids; ☎ (616) 456-3977.
Frederik Meijer Gardens, Grand Rapids; ☎ (616) 957-1580.
Gerald R. Ford Museum, Grand Rapids, ☎ (616) 451-9263.
John Ball Park & Zoo, Grand Rapids; ☎ (616) 336-4300.

Travel information
Grand Rapids/Kent County Visitors Bureau, ☎ (616) 459-8287 or (800) 678-9859, *www. visitgr.org*.
Kent County Park Commission ☎ (616) 774-3697.

11 Musketawa Trail

Trip Card

Starting point: Marne
Counties: Ottawa and Muskegon
Distance: 26 miles
Terrain: flat
Highlights: farmland, paved path,
Ravenna
Suggested riders: beginners

The Musketawa Trail is a slice of Americana. Originally the Central Michigan Railroad, the rail bed was acquired in 1992 and turned into a 27-mile rail-trail through the efforts of the Friends of the Musketawa Trail.

Today the 13-mile paved portion of the trail is only a 20-minute drive from the heart of Grand Rapids and provides weary urban dwellers with a country respite. Cyclists can park near the village of Marne, hop on the Musketawa Trail and journey back in time by comfortably cruising past quintessential Americana farms.

It's a flat path, where on a hot July morning cardinals swoop past the trail, rabbits scoot across and butterflies collect on wildflowers, all against a backdrop of rural Michigan. The scenery from the trail includes cornfields, red barns and small towns with farm implement stores. The trail also features 13 wooden trestles and a large observation deck overlooking Crockery Creek near Ravenna.

The paved portion extends from Marne to Ravenna, a nice halfway point on a 26-mile roundtrip journey. Not far off the trail is Ravenna's business district with a grocery store, deli and a couple of pizza parlors. As with most rail-trails, this flat and paved path is a ride that can be enjoyed by cyclists of almost any ability.

Those with mountain bikes or hybrids can ride another 14 miles towards Muskegon on a dirt and cinder surface. Future plans call for eventually paving the entire trail. For a map call the Ottawa County Parks and Recreation Commission at ☎ (616) 738-4810.

Stage One (6.7 miles) The trailhead in Marne is reached from I-96 by departing at exit 23 and heading north on 8th Avenue to a staging area just north of Garfield Road with parking, toilets and a picnic table. From the Marne trailhead the trail journeys northwest before swinging due west for Muskegon. Near *Mile 3* you reach the first wooden trestle and the second at *Mile 4.2*. The trail passes through farm country but is well shaded at times by large trees that are a pleasant contrast to the open fields. At *Mile 6.7* you arrive at the village of Conklin. The Conklin Store, open seven days a week, is right across the street from a grain elevator. Conklin also has a staging area with parking and toilets.

Stage Two (6.3 miles) Continue west on the trail and at *Mile 9.6* the trail passes from Ottawa County into Muskegon County. On this stretch off trail you cross several streets including a few gravel roads. The traffic is usually light but at *Mile 11* you do cross the Ravenna Road. ⚠ *Caution: This is the busiest crossing of the ride as you near the town of Ravenna.*

The highlight of this route is reached at *Mile 11.8*, the site of a 200-foot long trestle over Crockery Creek. Next to it is an observation deck with a picnic table large enough for a dinner party for your 12 best friends. Take a well deserved break and enjoy the view. Just past *Mile 12* you reach another staging area at Blackmer Road with toilets and parking. The pavement ends abruptly here but adventurous mountain bikers can cruise the rest of the way almost to Muskegon. For an energy stop in Ravenna, follow the food and drink signs to the gas stations, restaurants and a pizza parlor in town.

Stage Three (13 miles) Being a point-to-point trail the only way to return is to backtrack the way you came. If you're lucky you'll enjoy the wind at your back to cycle back smoothly in record time.

Bicycle sales, service

Cycle Therapy, 411 Wilson Ave. NW, Walker; ☎ (616) 791-0050.

North Kent Schwinn, 4336 Plainfield Ave. NE, Grand Rapids; ☎ (616) 363-0705.

Musketawa Trail

131

Dangle Rd.

26 miles

Cloverville

Mill Iron Rd.

Maple Island Rd.

Cleveland Rd.

State Rd.

Unpaved

Evanston Rd.

S. Moorland Rd.

Ellis Rd.

13 miles

68th Ave.

Blackmer Ave.

96

56th Ave.

Squires Rd.

Ravenna

Paved

40th Ave.

6.7 miles

Arthur Rd.

Conklin

Harding Rd.

Gooding Rd.

N

Marne

24th Ave.

Roosevelt Rd.

16th Ave.

Wilson Rd.

8th Ave.

Start 0.0
Finish 26 miles

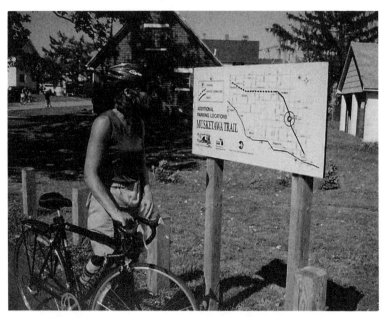

A cyclist studies a map along the Musketawa Trail

The Bicycle Rack, 1790 Roberts St., Muskegon; ☎ (231) 773-6411.

Breakaway Bicycles, 2145 W. Sherman Boulevard, Muskegon; ☎ (231) 759-0001.

Area events and festivals

May: Trillium Festival, Hoffmaster State Park, Muskegon.

June: Festival of the Arts, Grand Rapids; Lumbertown Music Festival, Muskegon.

September: Celebration on the Grand, Grand Rapids.

Travel information

Coopersville Chamber of Commerce, ☎ (616) 837-9731, *www.coopersville.com*.

Grand Rapids/Kent County Visitors Bureau, ☎ (616) 459-8287; (800) 678-9859, *www.visitgr.org*.

Friends of the Musketawa Trail, c/o Harold Drake, 3734 Center St., Ravenna, MI 49451.

12 Apple Country

Trip Card

Starting point: Alpine Township
County: Kent
Distance: 29.6 miles
Shorter option: 16.2 miles
Terrain: rolling hills, light traffic
Highlights: apple orchards, Sparta, fruit stands
Suggested riders: intermediate

"The Ridge," a little-known area in the northwest portion of Kent County and a part of Ottawa County, is blessed with hilly terrain and the proper distance from Lake Michigan that makes an ideal apple growing climate. It's the main reason Kent County grows more apples than any other county in Michigan. Rolling hills and scenic orchards also make this route a cyclist's dream.

From the days of annual apple smorgasbords which attracted national food writers, and 40 years of apple queens, the region is rich in tradition and loaded with apples. Today, the apple queens and smorgasbords may be gone but the bountiful apple harvest is still around and every fall people bite into such varieties as Ida Red, Macintosh, Jonathan, Delicious, Golden Delicious, Rome, Northern Spy, Winesap and Granny Smith along with little-known apples like Fuji and Gala. Harvesting the orchards is a group of down-to-earth, friendly folk, who have a passion for the land. It's not uncommon for a fifth-generation apple grower to be managing the family orchards.

Bicyclists will delight in this refreshing 29.6-mile journey that winds through the heart of apple country and past a half-dozen centennial farms. The ride begins appropriately at the Alpine Township Hall, on Alpine Avenue, northwest of Grand Rapids. Early May is an ideal time to journey through apple country as the blossoms are on the verge of bursting and often the temperature will be a comfortable mid-60s with slight breezes cooling you off at the top of the hills. Hills??? The beauty of these hills is that most of the time you'll have enough forward momentum going down to get you back up the next one. There's only one "thigh-burner," on Baumhoff Avenue coming back, but what's a ride without at least one hard, steep hill to help work up a good appetite.

Over halfway through the ride, you'll end up in downtown Sparta, a town of over 3,300 residents. Sparta is far enough (15 miles) away from the Grand Rapids metropolitan area to have its own identity and atmosphere. On your way out of Sparta, there's a fruit and vegetable stand, Bergman's, just one of many fruit stands and U-pick farms in the area. The Bergmans began selling fruit from their front porch in the 1930's.

You'll keep the power shopper in your group happy with this tour. Before or after your ride, you and your family can shop on Alpine Avenue, a strip that's become a mega-store area for discount and bargain shopping. Of course, there are restaurants here as well; Village Inn Pizza, Mr. Fables and Dairy Queen while hundreds more are not that far away in the greater Grand Rapids area.

Stage One (8.1 miles) Park in the Alpine Township Hall parking lot at 841 Alpine Church Rd., on the corner of Alpine Avenue (M-37) and Alpine Church Road. Head west on Alpine Church Road and at *Mile 1.5* turn right (north) on Baumhoff Avenue and pedal north until you reach 7 Mile Road at *Mile 3.* Turn left (west) on 7 Mile Road and shortly you'll pass the Alpine Historic Township Hall and Museum (☎ 616-785-0205). It's open the third Sunday of each month for those who want to step back into the history of this apple-growing region.

Continue west on 7 Mile Road and at *Mile 6* turn right (north) onto Stage Avenue. Stage Avenue is a scenic stretch with woodlots to the west and orchards so close on the right you can practically pick a bushel while pedaling through. Before heading east on 9 Mile Road, you can take a break by staying on Stage Avenue which quickly swings past Cranberry Lake, a small lake, half in Ottawa County and half in Kent County.

Stage Two (7.7 miles) From Stage Avenue, turn right (east) on 9 Mile Road and travel for 1.5 miles and then turn left (north) on Peach Ridge Avenue at *Mile 9.6.* Until the late 1920s, farmers grew

Just a few of the many bushels of apples and pears available at many of the farm markets in Kent County.

a lot of peaches in this area, now it's mostly apples and a few scattered peach trees, but the name of the road remained. On Peach Ridge Avenue, you head north for six miles. Unlike most lakeshore routes, the roads on the Apple Country Tour are straight, laid out in true directions of a compass. Roads such a 7, 9 and 15 Mile Roads make it easy for cyclists to know how far they have gone. Others, like Apple Ridge, Peach Ridge and Fruit Ridge, remind you where you are.

Stage Three (4.1 miles) From Peach Ridge Avenue, turn right on 15 Mile Road, at *Mile 15.8*, and head for two miles to Sparta Avenue. Turn right on Sparta Avenue and it's two more miles into downtown Sparta. ⚠ *Caution: This stretch has the most traffic, although it's lighter on weekends.* Sparta is a town with a mix of neighborhoods and its share of small industry. But apples are what Sparta is best known for and what the town actively promotes.

Stage Four (9.7 miles) Head south out of Sparta on Sparta

Avenue to M-37 (Alpine Avenue). ⚠ *M-37 is often a busy highway that has to be carefully crossed to reach 10 Mile Road on the west side.* Head right (west) on 10 Mile Road and in less than a mile you'll reach a picturesque Church of Christ at Ballard's Corner. Turn left (south) on Baumhoff Avenue to end the day with a rolling five-mile ride back to Alpine Church Road. Beware: there's one "thigh-burner" on this final stretch. From Baumhoff Avenue, turn left (east) on Alpine Church Street to return to the starting point at the Alpine Township Hall. You will pass Holy Trinity Catholic Church, nestled in a pretty (spiritual?) setting on your right, with a quiet cemetery across the road.

Shorter Option For a 16-mile loop, head west on Alpine Church Street and turn right (north) on Baumhoff Avenue. Turn left (west) on 7 Mile Road and then right (north) on Stage Avenue. Cycle to 9 Mile Road and turn right (east). But instead of heading north on Peach Ridge Avenue, continue on 9 Mile Road to Baumhoff Avenue. Turn right (south) on Baumhoff Avenue to Alpine Church Street and a quicker return to the starting point at the Alpine Township Hall.

Bicycle sales, service
Freewheeler Bike Shop, 915 Leonard St. NW, Grand Rapids; ☎ (616) 451-8011.

Alpine Cyclery, 3150 Alpine Ave. NW, Walker; ☎ (616) 785-0505.

North Kent Schwinn, 4336 Plainfield Ave. NE; Grand Rapids; ☎ (616) 363-0705.

Area events and festivals
June: Grand Rapids Festival of the Arts.
July: Sparta Town & Country Days.
September: Celebration on the Grand, Grand Rapids.
October: Pulaski Days, Grand Rapids.

Travel information
Sparta Area Chamber of Commerce; ☎ (616) 887-2454.
Grand Rapids/Kent County Visitors Bureau; ☎ (616) 459-8287 or (800) 678-9859, *www.visitgrandrapids.org.*

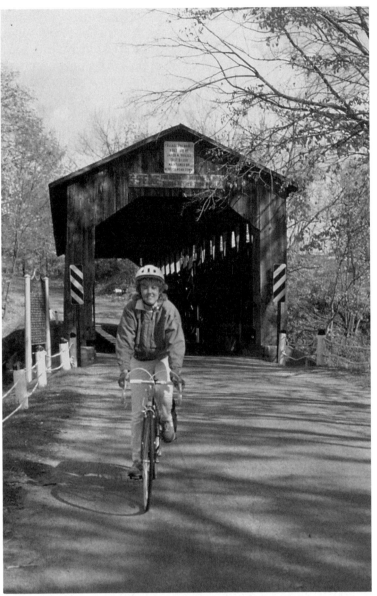

A cyclist crosses the Fallasburg Covered Bridge that was built in 1871 at a cost of $1,500.

13 Fallasburg Fun

Trip Card

Starting point: Fallasburg Park
County: Kent
Distance: 28.6 miles
Shorter option: 8 to 10 miles
Terrain: hilly
Highlights: Fallasburg Covered
Bridge, St. Patrick's Catholic Church,
Seidman Park
Suggested riders: advanced for longer loop,
beginners for shorter loop

Fallasburg Park, located north of Lowell in Kent County, is an ideal starting point for a bike ride. Known best for its historical covered bridge, the park is appropriately named because fall is the most spectacular time of year to visit the area. You not only get to enjoy the changing colors but you can also participate in the many events staged during autumn.

Riders of varying abilities will enjoy the 458-acre park which has fishing, nature trails and play equipment. Beginning cyclists may want to just ride the short distance to Lowell and back and then wait at one of the many scenic picnic spots while others grind out the 28.5 loop. This longer circuit heads north out of the park, works its way east to Parnell, then south to Ada before looping back to the park. On this jaunt you'll enjoy an excellent workout and wonderful scenery which will soothe your city-frazzled nerves. The latter half of the loop is particularly hilly with hills that roll and wind and don't want to level out by any means!

The highlight of the tour is the Fallasburg Historic Covered Bridge. Built in 1871 for $1,500, the bridge is undoubtedly the most photographed in the state. The long wooden structure is used each year in late June as part of the Multiple Sclerosis Bikeathon from Grand Rapids to Lansing. The bikeathon is a beautiful sight - hundreds of brightly-clad cyclists journeying over the wooden bridge. Across from the bridge is the Fallasburg Schoolhouse Museum. The country school, built in the 1860's, is open weekends from Memorial Day to mid-October.

Just five miles away near Smyrna, but not a part of this circuit, is White's Bridge. Built in 1867, this covered bridge also spans the Flat River. Also nearby, but not on the bike loop, is the Ada Covered Bridge which crosses the Thornapple River in Ada. This bridge, for pedestrians only, was built in 1867 and rebuilt in 1980 after a fire burned the original structure.

The countryside on this stretch is beautiful with many convenient places to stop. More than half the loop is a county-designated bicycle route, featuring wide shoulders. There are a couple of small stores with bathroom facilities, and places for refreshments on Parnell Road. When we toured the area, we stopped and admired the stately St. Patrick's Catholic Church, a centennial building that was built in 1877. Its steeple is visible for miles and can be seen while traveling west on Parnell Road.

There are also two parks and lakes where you can stop and rest and admire the beauty: Townsend Park, 13 miles into the loop, and Seidman Park at Mile 17.3. Only 20 miles from Grand Rapids, Lowell is renowned for its Showboat on the Flat River, an event held the third weekend in June featuring nationally known entertainers. The Flat River Antique Mall, in downtown Lowell, includes four floors of antiques and collectibles and it's open on Sundays too, making it a wonderful place to browse before or after your ride. In Lowell there are also many places for the hungry cyclist to eat.

Stage One (9.9 miles) This tour begins at Fallasburg Covered Bridge in Fallasburg Park, reached by driving north of Lowell on Lincoln Lake Avenue and following park signs. From the historic bridge head west on Covered Bridge Road back to Lincoln Lake Avenue. The first two miles will be a scenic jaunt along the park drive and then you turn right (north) on Lincoln Lake Avenue. You'll discover this road is relatively flat with nice wide shoulders and light traffic. At *Mile 6.8*, turn left (west) on Parnell Road (also labeled 5 Mile Road). Both Lincoln Lake Avenue and Parnell Road are designated county bike routes. Near *Mile 10* there's a small store

CANNONSBURG

TOWNSEND PARK

PARNELL

Five Mile Rd.

6.8 Miles

13 Miles

Lincoln Lake Ave.

Short loop • 10 Miles
Start • 0 Miles
Finish • 28.5 Miles

Two Mile Rd.

Honey Creek Ave.

SEIDMAN PARK

FALLSBURG PARK

17.3 Miles

Bailey Dr.

Bailey Dr.

27 Miles

LOWELL

across from the stately St. Patrick's Catholic Church and cemetery on Parnell Road. This is a leisurely place to take a refreshment break and savor the countryside. Remember to drink lots of liquids.

Stage Two (9.5 miles) Keep heading west on Parnell Road which veers northwest and turns into Cannonsburg Road, still part of the designated bike route. At *Mile 13*, on the corner of Cannonsburg Road and Honey Creek Avenue, there's Grist Mill Market and Pizza and the Honey Creek Inn, a quaint country bar and restaurant with imported beer on tap (in case anybody is still hungry from the last break) while just to the north is Townsend Park. This 157-acre county park has plenty of opportunities for fishing and hiking along the nature trails. From the park, head south on Honey Creek Avenue. Within a mile you return to a designated bike route. At *Mile 17.3* there's Seidman Park, a 422-acre unit with opportunities for hikers and anglers as well as cross country skiers in the winter. In a route of hilly terrain, there is one heart-pounding hill located at the end of stage two. Suck in a deep breath, put your head down and climb!

Stage Three (9.2 miles) From Honey Creek Avenue, turn left on Pettis Avenue and then make another quick left on Vergennes Street and immediately look for Bailey Drive, which veers off to the northeast. This is an odd intersection with four streets coming together by the Grand River. Shady Acres Farms, reached just before *Mile 24*, offers hayrides in a rustic country setting. Bailey Road winds past homes in picturesque settings as you tour 8.4 miles back to your final destination at Fallasburg Park. At *Mile 27* turn left (north) on Lincoln Lake Avenue and then right (east) on Fallasburg Park Drive to re-enter the park. Whew! Time to relax in the park, take pictures by the covered bridge, grill your dinner or head to Lowell to a local restaurant.

Shorter Option (8 to 10 miles) Cycle through Fallasburg Park and then turn left (south) on Lincoln Lake Avenue. From the entrance of the park, it's approximately four miles to the town of Lowell. You can cycle as far into town as you want to go before backtracking to the park.

Area attractions

June: Lowell Showboat, Lowell; ☎ (800) 422-SHOW, or (616) 897-8280.

August: Kent County Youth Fair, Lowell fairgrounds.

September: Alto Fall Festival, Alto; Fallasburg Fall Festival, Fallasburg Park.

Travel information

Lowell Area Chamber of Commerce; ☎ (616) 897-9161.

14 Squires Street

Trip Card

Starting point: Rockford
County: Kent
Distance: 26 miles
Shorter option: 11.4 miles
Terrain: rolling, hilly
Highlights: Wabasis Lake Park, Squires Street, Rogue River, Corner Bar
Suggested riders: intermediate to advanced

If you're looking for a miniature ceramic collie, a half pound of fresh-roasted coffee, quality second-hand clothing, baskets of all shapes and sizes, humorous birthday cards or hanging crystals for your window, you'll find it at the Squires Street Square, a diverse shopping area in downtown Rockford. This quaint town of 3,000 residents is 15 miles north of Grand Rapids and known as a shopper's paradise. But historic Rockford also serves as a good home base for a 26-mile bicycle route.

Rockford was founded in 1843 when a young entrepreneur named Smith Lapham purchased land along the Rogue River and then built a dam and saw mill. A shingle mill, grist mill and machine shop soon followed and by the late 1800s Rockford was a bustling commercial center with warehouses, a train depot, and a bean processing plant on the river.

The town then experienced a rebirth in the early 1970s when the bean warehouse was renovated into a cider mill, attracting both locals and visitors heading north. Eventually the sweet cider and even sweeter donuts of the Old Mill led to the shopping district of Squires Street Square, where today you'll find unique shops. Nearby is west Michigan's first outlet mall and the factory store of Wolverine World Wide, maker of Hush Puppies shoes.

Cycling West Michigan

This 26-mile bicycle route begins in the Squires Street area near the dam, an ideal resting place before or after your ride, where anglers can often be seen casting for steelhead and salmon. The route is a hilly, sometimes winding ride, through a mixture of open country, farms and stands of hardwoods. Wabasis Lake Park is an impressive area with a large shimmering lake. The Kent County park features a campground, beach and bathhouses. The park itself is quite hilly; so if you venture in be prepared to climb a couple of hills.

The return to Rockford on Summit Avenue is a fun, winding, downhill ride while the 11.4-mile loop option provides a taste of the surrounding area as well as the opportunity to cycle past two small lakes: Brower and Myers.

To motivate yourself up those lengthy hills along the loop, keep in mind the many fine eateries with a fresh table waiting for you at the finish in Rockford. Probably the most famous is the Corner Bar, 31 North Main St. (☎ 616-866-9866). Since 1965, the Corner Bar has not only been serving great hot dogs but is the site of the Hot Dog Hall of Fame. If you eat 12 hot dogs in four hours or less, you too can be inducted into this hall with your name engraved onto a brass plate on the wall. If you're seeking gastronomic fame, I recommend you try after your bike ride, not before. By the way, the record is 42-1/2 chili dogs consumed in a single sitting and is held by Sharon Scholten. There are many other fine restaurants in Rockford, including Vitale's Pizza, 42 E. Bridge St., (☎ 616-866-4467), and Arnie's Old Mill Restaurant, 34 Squires St., (☎ 616-866-4306).

Stage One (9.9 miles) The starting point is a parking area on East Bridge Street, near the Squires Street shops and the Rogue River dam. Turn left on East Bridge Street and then right on South Main Street, where Speed Merchants Bike Shop is on this corner for any last minute repairs. Turn left on East Division and head east out of town on 10 Mile Road where you'll soon pass a McDonalds restaurant (time to eat yet??)

This is a cardiovascular ride and you're tipped off to this by some steep hills early in the tour. A long hill is encountered near *Mile 2* and another after passing Myers Lake Avenue at *Mile 3.4*. Big Brower Lake will be seen to the north and then Ramsdell Drive at *Mile 6.4*. At *Mile 8.7* turn left (north) on Wabasis Avenue and look to your right for the Wabasis Lake Park reached just before *Mile 10*.

The 102-acre park is located on the west side of its namesake

9.9 Miles

Wabasis Rd.

N

WABASIS
PARK

8.7 Miles

12 Mile Rd.

14.9 Miles

Ramsdell Dr.

14 Mile Rd.

MYERS
LAKE
PARK

Myers Lake Ave.

Myers Lake Ave.

18 Miles

12 Mile Rd.

10 Mile Rd.

13 Mile Rd.

Short loop • 11.4

Start • 0 Miles

Finish • 26 Miles

22.8 Miles

Summit Ave.

ROCKFORD

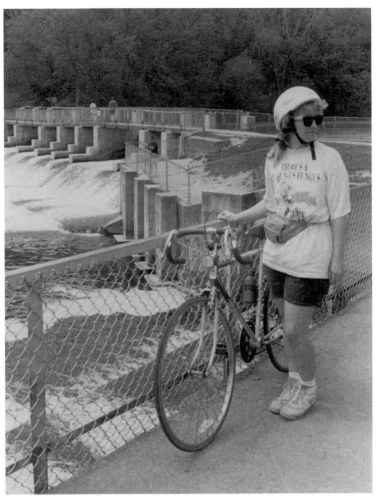

Cyclist on the Rockford Dam at the Rogue River.

lake and features several picnic areas with shelters, restrooms, water, a bathhouse, swimming beach and a small store in the campground. This is a good place to check out the activity on the lake, stretch your legs or munch on some treats you've packed.

Stage Two (9.2 miles) From the entrance to Wabasis Park, head north again on Wabasis Avenue where you immediately pass a parking lot for a scenic overlook above the lake. Near *Mile 11* turn left (west) onto 12 Mile Road and in two miles turn right (north) on Ramsdell Drive. After crossing Peterson Street at *Mile 13.4*, turn left (west) on 14 Mile Road (M-57) at *Mile 15.* ⚠ *Caution: This can be a busy highway, so another option is to turn left (west) on Peterson Street, though this would shorten the ride by three miles.* Follow M-57 for three miles then turn left (south) onto Myers Lake Avenue to reach 13 Mile Road and complete stage two and 19 miles of the tour.

Stage Three (7 miles) Head west on 13 Mile Road for four miles and then turn left (south) on Summit Avenue at *Mile 22.8*. Within a mile you'll arrive at a quirky intersection where you turn right (west) on 12 Mile Road and then make an immediate left (south) back onto Summit Avenue.

The final leg is a scenic and roguish stretch. You'll be cycling parallel to the Rogue River while descending back to the downtown area. At *Mile 25.2* the Rockford city limits is reached. Cross the river and turn left on Bridge Street to return to the starting point. It's time to browse for distinctive gifts and eat, or simply relax on the banks of the charming Rogue River, watching the canoeists or fishermen.

Shorter Option (11.4-mile) From 10 Mile Road, turn left (north) on Myers Lake Avenue to 12 Mile Road, where you turn left (west). Pedal four miles on 12 Mile Road to Summit Avenue where you turn left (south) to return to the starting point on East Bridge Street.

Bicycle sales, service

The Speed Merchants, corner of Main and Bridge Streets., Rockford; ☎ (616) 866-2226.

Area events and festivals

June: Start of Summer Festival, Rockford.

July: Old Fashioned Sidewalk Sales, Rockford.

September: Harvest Festival, Rockford (three weekends in September and October); Red Flannel Festival, Cedar Springs.

Travel information

Rockford Chamber of Commerce; ☎ (616) 866-2000, *www.grnet.com/rockfordcoc*.

Cedar Springs Chamber of Commerce; ☎ (616) 696-3260.

The Lake Michigan beach at Duck Lake State Park

15 ///// Blockhouse Hill /////

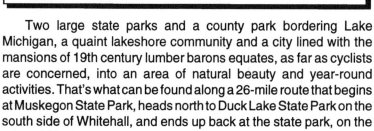

Trip Card

Starting point: Muskegon State Park
County: Muskegon
Distance: 26 miles
Shorter option: 12 miles
Terrain: varied terrain, hilly in the beginning
Highlights: Muskegon State Park, Lake Michigan, Duck Lake State Park
Suggested riders: intermediate

Two large state parks and a county park bordering Lake Michigan, a quaint lakeshore community and a city lined with the mansions of 19th century lumber barons equates, as far as cyclists are concerned, into an area of natural beauty and year-round activities. That's what can be found along a 26-mile route that begins at Muskegon State Park, heads north to Duck Lake State Park on the south side of Whitehall, and ends up back at the state park, on the edge of Muskegon.

Muskegon is blessed with another state park on its south side, P.J. Hoffmaster, known best for the Michigan Sand Dune Interpretive Center. But this bicycle route begins at Muskegon State Park, an equally impressive park just north of town. The loop, made up of lightly traveled roads and Lake Michigan scenery, offers plenty of opportunities to stop for quick swims and gourmet picnicking.

Don't panic during the first part of the loop; it's very hilly as you make your way out of Muskegon State Park along Scenic Drive. But the effort is definitely worth it, especially when you pause on top of Blockhouse Hill, where you can take in a panorama of the park's wooded interior, the dunes along Lake Michigan and even Muskegon

Lake. The route becomes easier after the first stage as you follow Lake Michigan to Duck Lake. Along the way you pass by out-of-the-way beaches, a family resort in Michillinda Beach Lodge near Whitehall and delightful cycling roads such as Michillinda Drive.

I pedaled this route on a day when temperatures were in the 80's. Yet I found the ride pleasant because the breezes off of Lake Michigan and the shady segments of the route compensated for the not-so-comfortable heat. The 12-mile option allows cyclists to see the lakeshore scenery as well as put in a short workout.

This Muskegon-Duck Lake circuit could be the first half of an excellent two-day outing with the second day spent pedaling the 22-mile Hart-Montague Bike Trail, Michigan's first linear state park. The rail-trail route (see page 119), begins in Montague, just 15 miles north of Muskegon.

To many, Muskegon is known as an industrial city on the lake, but in recent years tourism has taken on increased importance. There are many family attractions, including Michigan Adventure Amusement Park (☎ 231-766-3377), along with the state and county parks. Other Muskegon attractions include the Hackley and Hume Homes, restored lumber baron mansions, tours on the *USS Silversides*, a World War II submarine, and the *Port City Princess*, offering dinner and scenic cruises.

Fifteen miles north of the area are Muskegon's smaller cousins, Whitehall and Montague, pleasant resort communities on White Lake. There are some neat options for dining here, such as the Crosswinds Restaurant on White Lake. Along the route there are some excellent ice cream stops, or you can grill your dinner back at the state park. The Bear Lake Inn, featuring a fun, casual atmosphere in North Muskegon near the start of the bike route, is also a good place to eat.

Stage One (9.2 miles) From the beach parking area in Muskegon State Park, head north on Scenic Drive. Oh, the hills! But the view makes it worth the effort especially when you reach the Blockhouse halfway through the park. The original Blockhouse was built by the CCC in 1935 but burned down in 1962. The replica was constructed two years later and from its second floor you can see the park's highpoint, a wooded dune at 792 feet, while to the west is the blue horizon of Lake Michigan and to the southeast Muskegon Lake.

At *Mile 2* you'll depart the park and enter a shady neighborhood with Lake Michigan to the west. Cross Giles Road at *Mile 2.7*, a slightly busy corner, and within a quarter mile you'll reach Pioneer County Park, a popular area for camping and sunbathing. The Red Rooster Tavern is passed at *Mile 5.6* and is followed by a long stretch of shaded road where the lake breezes provide a comfortable break from the summer heat. There's a small township park to

The Blockhouse at Muskegon State Park.

the west at *Mile 7.5* that provides more access to the beach.

At *Mile 8* you reach a interesting passage between two bodies of water. On your right is Duck Lake with a boardwalk leading to an inland beach and picnic area. On your left is Lake Michigan with another beach beneath a towering dune. Both are part of Duck Lake State Park, a 728-acre unit that was dedicated in 1988. The park is a day-use facility with no campground, but arrive on a Saturday in July and you'll be impressed by the dune...and the large number of people spread out on the beach. By *Mile 9* you pass the Michillinda Beach Lodge, an old-fashioned resort with a modified American Plan (some meals, lodging, and use of all facilities included in one price) on Lake Michigan as well as a party store, where you can take a refreshment break. At *Mile 9.2*, turn right (east) on Michillinda Drive.

Stage Two (9.8 miles) Head east on Michillinda Drive and at *Mile 10.3* you'll pass the entrance of Duck Lake State Park. You'll certainly appreciate the wide shoulders on this road before turning right (south) on Orshal Road at *Mile 12*. A long uphill segment is encountered at *Mile 12.8* and within a half mile you turn left (east) on Duck Lake Road. Cycle three miles and then turn right (south) on Lorenson Road. This road features farm country with picturesque barns. The second stage ends by turning right (west) on River Road.

Stage Three (7 miles) After turning on River Road, you immediately turn left (south) on Buys Road at *Mile 19.2*. Within a mile you reach the Maple Ridge Historic School, a one-room structure. Turn right at *Mile 21.4* onto Fenner Road which will lead back into the Muskegon State Park. The Blockhouse is on your left at *Mile 25*, if you didn't stop there on your way out. The ride ends at *Mile 26* in the middle of the Muskegon State Park.

Shorter Option (12 miles) Take Scenic Drive north for 4.4 miles and turn right (east) onto River Road. At *Mile 6.8* turn right on Peterson Road, a lightly traveled road with no shoulders. Cycle to Fenner Road at *Mile 9* and then turn right (west) to reach Scenic Road. Turn left (south) and you'll reach the starting point at the day-use area and beach in the center of the park.

Bicycle sales, service

The Bicycle Rack, 1790 Roberts Rd., Muskegon; ☎ (231) 773-6411.

Breakaway Bicycles, 2145 W. Sherman Boulevard, Muskegon; ☎ (231) 759-0001.

Rock 'N' Road Cycle, 300 N. 7th, Grand Haven; ☎ (231) 846-2800.

Area events and festivals

May: Trillium Festival, Hoffmaster State Park.

June: Lumbertown Festival, Muskegon; White Lake Area Arts and Crafts Festival, Whitehall.

August: White Lake Maritime Festival, Whitehall.

Travel information

Muskegon County Convention & Visitors Bureau, ☎ (231) 724-3100 or (800) 250-9283, *www.muskegon.org*.

White Lake Area Chamber of Commerce, ☎ (231) 893-4585 or (800) 879-9702, *www.whitelake.org*.

Muskegon State Park, ☎ (231) 744-3480.

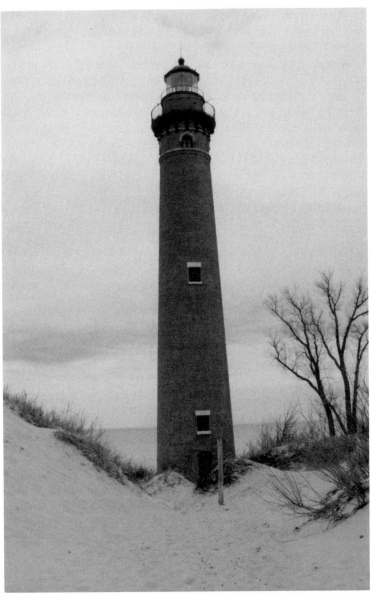

One of most interesting attractions in Silver Lake State Park is Little Point Sable Lighthouse, which was built in 1874.

16 Silver Lake Amble

Trip Card

Starting point: Silver Lake
County: Oceana
Distance: 25 miles
Shorter option: 5 miles
Terrain: mostly flat, some hills inland
Highlights: shifting sand dunes,
Silver Lake State Park, fruit markets
Suggested riders: intermediate

They call the dunes of Silver Lake State Park Michigan's own Sahara Desert. The 2,800-acre unit is another Lake Michigan park, with 1,800 acres of it forming a mile-wide strip between the Great Lake and Silver Lake. Even for the dune country of west Michigan this area is unique. Its ridges and valleys are mostly wind-blown sand, lacking trees, scrub, or even dune grass, forming steep-side mountains of shifting sand.

The dunes, the park and all the side attractions of the area, ranging from dune buggy rides to water slides, attracts hordes of visitors every summer. But the area also makes a logical starting point for a pleasant 25-mile cycling route that begins at Silver Lake State Park. The ride heads south out of the hustle and bustle of tourists and away from the strips of restaurants, resorts and camp-grounds and quickly takes you into open farm and orchard country.

You'll quickly discover on this ride that Oceana County is a major fruit and vegetable-growing area. More tart cherries are grown here than any other county in the United States, including Grand Traverse County, Michigan's so-called cherry country. Then there is the asparagus! There's so much grown here that the towns of Hart and Shelby put on an annual Asparagus Festival that is highlighted with the crowning of the Asparagus Queen. I'm not kidding.

There's the Cherry Point Farm Market, reached four miles into the tour, for a wide range of cherry and fruit products, and then the ride heads east, close to Shelby before looping back through Mears and the Silver Lake area.

This Silver Lake loop could also be easily combined with the 22-mile Hart-Montague Trail (see page 119) for a longer ride or a weekend of cycling, as this route intersects the Hart-Montague Trail at two different points.

Those with extra time before or after the ride will enjoy the natural features of Silver Lake State Park. The dunes have been divided into three separate areas with small sections at the north end designated for ORVs and the south end for a dune-ride concession. Mac Wood's Dune Rides (☎ 231-873-2817) offers rides on 12-passenger open truck-like "dune scooters." The Wood family has been riding the sands for 60 years, entertaining visitors with a bit of history and folklore, while zigzagging up, over and around the dunes.

The majority of the dunes in the middle is a pedestrian area. Here visitors depart their cars (or bicycles) and take to the Sahara Desert on foot in a mile-long trek to the beautiful and uncrowded beaches along Lake Michigan. Equally interesting is the Little Point Sable Lighthouse at the south end of the park. Built in 1874, the lighthouse is still maintained by the Coast Guard but is best known as one of the most scenic places to watch a sunset over Lake Michigan. The lighthouse day-use area is reached by continuing west where Scenic Drive (also County Road B15) turns south at the Mac Woods Dune Rides and following the signs along the narrow dirt road, perfect on a mountain bike.

Of course any place that attracts this many summer tourists, must serve ice cream by the ton...one scoop at a time. Overheated cyclists will appreciate several places on "the strip", including Whippy Dip (home of the famous turtle sundae) near the state park and soft and hard ice cream at the Sands Restaurant.

Stage One (3.2 miles) From Silver Lake State Park, head south on Scenic Drive but be careful; the road can be very busy with cars, pedestrians and bike traffic. You'll pass cottages on both sides and within a mile the road curves to the left (south) at 18th Avenue. On the corner is Mac Wood's Dune Rides followed by the Whippy Dip, which serves the best soft serve on this tourist strip. For those on mountain bikes, you can continue straight for a side trip to the lighthouse, an extra 3 miles at this point. Little Sable Point Light-house is one of the most photographed in the state even though the adjoining lightkeeper's house was demolished in 1954, leaving only the conical tower. But at 108 feet in height, it's one of the tallest on the west side of the state and requires 145 steps to reach the lens at the top.

The tour, meanwhile, heads south on 18th Avenue (also labeled County Road B15 on maps), a fairly wide road that is lightly travelled. You pass through farm country and apple orchards and pedal segments that are lined by ancient oaks or maples and painted in early summer by wildflowers. At *Mile 3* 18th Avenue curves to the right (west) and merges into Buchanan Road at this point. More orchards are passed and at *Mile 3.2* Cherry Point Farm Market is reached. Snack time! The market is open seven days a week, selling homemade cherry pies, bread, baked goods, jams and jelly, hot or cold drinks as well as a selection of country crafts and gifts. It's a friendly place to stop for a quick break or load up your bike bag with snacks for later.

Stage Two (11.3 miles) From Cherry Point Farm Market, the road curves sharply to your left (south) and becomes 16th Avenue, (still called Scenic Drive and County Road B15). You'll struggle over a hill at *Mile 4.4* and then within a third mile turn left (east) on Shelby Road. Shelby Road is a pleasant mixture of stands of pines and hardwoods, faded red barns, wildflowers and orchards. There's a long, but gradual uphill section beginning at *Mile 7* followed by more fertile orchards and trees. In the next two miles you'll cycle past a slice of rural Michigan; including large wooden barns and silos and a centennial farm with a bulky stone porch.

A hilly section is encountered at *Mile 9.5* before the road levels out and you eventually cross the US-31 overpass. At *Mile 11.8* turn left (north) on 72nd Street, located just west of the town of Shelby. This road immediately heads downhill, curving to the right and is a narrow but lightly traveled avenue. You pass horse stables and encounter more hills, including a steep one at *Mile 12.5* reached just before you intersect the Hart-Montague Trail. Stay on 72nd Avenue and guess what? More orchards and hills! This stretch is the most rolling portion of the Silver Lake route and begins with a steep incline at *Mile 14* followed by an equally long downhill ride (ahhhhh!). You'll pass Baseline Road at *Mile 14.5* to complete stage two.

Stage Three (10.5 miles) Just north of Baseline Road, 72nd Avenue becomes a well, shaded route and then at *Mile 15* swings west to skirt around Crystal Lake, a small lake with a few cottages. Just after Scout Road merges from the east, there's a public access site on the lake, a pleasant spot if your tired legs need a break.

At Crystal Lake the road turns into 68th Avenue and is followed by another long, steep hill, past Duck Road, at *Mile 15.3.* Straight ahead you come to the junction and stop sign on Taylor Road where nearby a dilapidated church sits. Swing right (east) on Taylor and then left (north) back on 72nd Avenue where a gradual hill is encountered at *Mile 16.8* followed by a mix of hardwoods and orchards that pleasantly line the road.

You intersect the Hart-Montague Trail again at *Mile 17.5* just before turning left (west) on Polk Road. This is a busy road, but features wide shoulders on both sides. Within a half mile you'll pass

✿✿✿✿✿✿✿✿✿✿✿✿✿✿✿✿✿✿✿✿✿✿

Adding Miles To The Silver Lake Amble

This 25-mile route can be easily lengthened by cycling further east on Shelby Road into Shelby and cycling further north to Hart before heading back west to Silver Lake. Also keep in mind that to the north, Pentwater (a Silver Lake with more class), is a worthwhile destination. This popular resort town has a state park, many eateries and unique shops. Pentwater can be reached from Silver Lake by heading north on Hazel Road to Ridge Avenue, which you follow into town.

✿✿✿✿✿✿✿✿✿✿✿✿✿✿✿✿✿✿✿✿✿✿

over US-31 a second time and then head due west as Polk Road narrows down to two lanes. Turn left (south) on 56th Avenue at *Mile 19.6* and then right (west) in a half mile on 4th Avenue (also called Hazel Road). Soon you'll enter the small town of Mears, a good place to stop for a breather before returning to Silver Lake.

Named after a west Michigan lumber baron, Mears has a grocery store, restaurant and antique shops. It's also the home of the Mears Newz bulletin board that is changed on a regular basis by local citizens. Residents invite you to stop and check out "What's ripe in the Land of Mears!" The Oceana County Museum in Mears was once the home of Swift Lathers, who published the Mears Newz for more than 50 years as the world's smallest newspaper. Just south of the town, the Hart-Montague Trail passes by.

From Mears, Fox Road heads west to the Silver Lake area, passing through a tunnel of trees at Mile *21.8* and another farmer's market at *Mile 23*. In another quarter mile you reach the junction and stop sign at County Road B15. Turn left (south) and you'll quickly notice the brown and white Oceana Circle Tour signs that complement the Lake Michigan Circle Tour signs on federal and state highways. CR-B15 curves sharply to your right at *Mile 23.6* followed by another right-hand curve as it enters the Silver Lake area curving again to the right. You can see water straight ahead at *Mile 24*. You will also see the flashing neon signs advertising for restaurants, miniature golf, T-shirt shops, ice cream parlours, campgrounds and other tourist trappings before you reach your starting point, the entrance of the Silver Lake State Park at *Mile 25*.

Shorter Option (2-4 miles) The road following Silver Lake has bike route signs and is a leisurely ride for beginners or cyclists who want an off-day. The portion of the road on the north side of Silver Lake is especially nice, with less congestion and ample shoulders. You can cycle as far as you want to go and then backtrack to your motel room or campground.

Area events and festivals
June: Asparagus Festival, Hart/Shelby.

July: Arts & Crafts Fair, Pentwater; Fourth of July fireworks, Silver Lake.

Area attractions
Craig's Cruisers Fun Park, Mears; ☎ (231) 873-2511.
Mac Wood's Dune Rides, Mears; ☎ (231) 873-2817.
Sandy Korners ORV Rental, Mears; ☎ (231) 873-5048

Travel information
Hart/Silver Lake Chamber of Commerce; ☎ (231) 873-2247, *www.oceana.net*.

Silver Lake Tourist Association; ☎ (231) 873-5018.
Silver Lake State Park; ☎ (231) 833-3083.

17 Hart-Montague Trail

Trip Card

Starting point: Hart
Counties: Oceana and Muskegon
Distance: 22 miles
Shorter option: 8 miles
Terrain: flat, asphalt trail
Highlights: Whitehall/Montague,
Shelby, Mears, Hart, trailside parks
Suggested riders: beginners

Some friends and I discovered the Hart-Montague Bicycle Trail, Michigan's first linear state park, a decade ago and it's been a special place to us ever since. Located in Oceana County, a land of tart cherries, apples, picture-postcard farms and beautiful waterways; this trail offers a sampling of what West Michigan is all about.

The rail trail connects the John Gurney Park in Hart with the southern trailhead in Montague, passing along the way clusters of wildflowers, small-town train depots, and inviting ice cream stands. What makes the trail so special is the feeling you get when you're on it. The ambience of nature combined with a small-town escape, away from the city, is the best part of the adventure. I suspect it's what train passengers felt when the trail was part of the Chicago and West Michigan Railroad, a line that was built in 1872 to connect Pentwater to Grand Rapids.

The communities along the Hart-Montague have enhanced the trail with parks, parking areas and other amenities. The successful completion of the trail in 1990 has been a catalyst to the Rails-to-Trails movement to develop other proposed trails from abandoned rail lines throughout Michigan. In fact, the state has a special grant program for development of trails that link communities through the conversion of abandoned railroads.

Cycling West Michigan

The asphalt trail, a little over 22 miles long, begins in Hart and travels along the former C&O Railroad that was abandoned in 1981. This rail bed is flat, yet passes through rolling terrain of beautiful hills and valleys. The best part, of course, is the absence of auto traffic and that makes for a relaxing ride.

This bike trail is a great tour for large groups of cyclists. I once rode the trail with more than 15 other cyclists of all ages, including toddlers and pre-teens. All of us met in Shelby, (Mile 8 of the trail), and naturally broke off into groups according to our speed. Some went 10 miles, others went 44 miles, pedaling the entire point-to-point trail then backtracking. Non-cyclists in your group can drop you off at the beginning and then spend the afternoon in Hart or better yet the Montague/Whitehall area, while waiting for you to finish the ride.

Montague and Whitehall, twin cities at the southern trailhead and home to just over 5,000 people, are the largest communities along the trail. The towns, located on the White River and White Lake, which empty into Lake Michigan, feature a nautical atmosphere. Much of their seafaring history can be seen at the White River Light Station Museum (☎ 231-894-8265) built in 1875 overlooking Lake Michigan.

Hungry after your trail adventure? Try the Crosswinds Restaurant, just down the hill from downtown Whitehall, overlooking White Lake. It's a casual sit-down place, (accessible even by boat), and it's known for its fresh fish. For terrific deli sandwiches and hand-dipped ice cream, go to Pekadill's, 503 S. Mears Avenue in Whiteall. In Hart, the locals recommended the LaFiesta Mexican Food Restaurant as a good dining spot.

During the summer Whitehall and Montague have several art fairs while nearby Blue Lake Fine Arts Camp (seven miles east of Whitehall in Twin Lake) offers a full schedule of summer concerts, ranging from small jazz ensembles to orchestras. A unique attraction in Shelby is Shelby Man-Made Gemstones (☎ 231-861-2165), which manufactures and sells man-made diamonds, rubies, sapphires and emeralds. There's a showroom with interpretive displays and an audio-visual theater.

For those who want to combine camping and cycling there's Hart's John Gurney Park. The modern campground has 104 sites on Hart Lake and is ideally located near the beginning of the trail.

Trail Fee The linear state park is also an excellent tune-up for

HART

MONTAGUE

the biking season, a good way to put in 44 miles, on a flat, fast surface. Being a state park there is, however, a user fee for cycling on the trail. The required trail passes can be purchased at various businesses along the trail, including Cherry Valley Hardware in Hart, or the Country Variety Convenience Store in New Era. Or they can be obtained from park rangers who patrol the trail. The passes are available on a daily or annual basis for individuals or families.

Stage One (8 miles) From the trailhead near John Gurney Park, head south on the asphalt trail to begin what many feel is most scenic of the two halves. The trail quickly passes through town and swings southwest, where in less than a mile, it crosses Polk Road, part of the Silver Lake route (see page 113). You'll cycle under US-31 at *Mile 1.3* and then at *Mile 2.5* have the opportunity to depart the trail north for a short side trip into Mears. The small village is an interesting place with small shops and more great places to eat!

Back on the trail, just before *Mile 3*, you'll find the first of three picnic areas with tables located near the trail. From this "cycler's rest area," the trail winds its way eastward, crossing Baseline Road and Buchanan Road before you reach the town of Shelby at *Mile 8*.

In Shelby (population 1,624), the trail jogs behind Michigan Avenue, which is the town's business district. There are several places to eat nearby such as the Pizza Factory (☎ 231-861-5036), the Wooden Nickel Restaurant (☎ 231-861-5910) or the Fireplug Restaurant (☎ 231-861-2300), which serves Hudsonville ice cream. For those with a bike bag full of food, Getty Field is about a block from the trail and has a source of water while Memorial Park is two blocks from the former depot downtown.

Stage Two (4 miles) From Shelby, the trail heads south, crossing Baker Road at *Mile 9* and then Grant Road. The only wooden trestle on the trail is located between Shelby and New Era. The small town of New Era is reached at *Mile 12* of the route and features a trailside park specially designed for Hart-Montague Trail users. Here you'll find a very nice shelter, restrooms and a scenic bridge over a small stream. This is not only a very pleasant spot but you're also halfway to Montague. Time for an extended break.

Stage three (10 miles) From New Era, the trail makes a beeline to Montague, closely paralleling Oceana Drive almost the entire way. You cross Arthur Road at *Mile 13* and then Cleveland Road shortly after that. At *Mile 15*, you reach Rothbury, where you'll find a picnic area, restrooms, water and play equipment - in case your children are not already worn out from the ride. From Rothbury, it's a quick seven miles to the end of the trail in Montague. Along the way keep an eye out for bluebird boxes attached to trees.

At the southern trailhead, located near Old US-31 and Stanton Boulevard in Montague, there is a special parking area for trail users, a small pavilion and restrooms.

Shorter Option (8 miles) With plenty of parking areas near the trail, there are many shorter trail options. A nice eight-mile option is to start in Shelby and head south to New Era before doubling back.

Bicycle sales, service
Rothbury Hardware & Farm Supply, ☎ (231) 861-2418.

Travel information
June: Asparagus Festival, Hart & Shelby; White Lake Area Arts & Crafts Festival, Whitehall.
August: White Lake Maritime Festival, Whitehall.

Area attractions
Shelby Man Made Gems, Shelby; ☎ (231) 861-2165.
White River Light Station Museum; ☎ (231) 894-8265.

Travel information
Silver Lake State Park; ☎ (231) 873-3083.
White Lake Area Chamber of Commerce; ☎ (231) 893-4585, *www.whitelake.org*.
Hart/Silver Lake Chamber of Commerce; ☎ (231) 873-2247, *www.oceana.net*.
Shelby Chamber of Commerce; ☎ (231) 861-4054.
New Era Chamber of Commerce; ☎ (231) 861-5219.

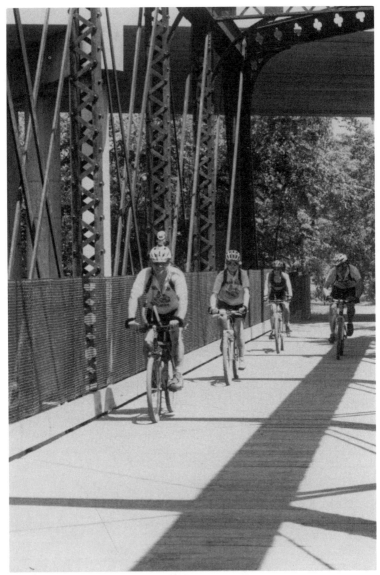

Cyclists cross Whites Bridge over the Muskegon River along the White Pine Trail. At 319 feet the bridge is the longest on the trail.

18 White Pine Trail

Trip Card

Starting point: Big Rapids
Counties: Mecosta, Osceola
Distance: 26 miles
Terrain: flat, converted railbed
Highlights: Muskegon River,
Paris Park
Suggested riders: beginners

When Michigan's rails to trails movement took off, the 92-mile White Pine Trail quickly became a dream and then slowly reality. The trail, dedicated in 1995, stretches 92 miles from Comstock Park near Grand Rapids and journeys northward along the former Michigan Northern of the Penn Central Railroad to Cadillac.

Currently only the 5.5-mile stretch from Belmont to 12 Mile Road north of Rockford and a 13-mile stretch from Big Rapids to Reed City are paved. Anyone who has ever journeyed north of Grand Rapids on US 131 will discover that the White Pine Trail is a similar - though quieter - corridor through the back door of many small communities. You'll cross the Grand and Rogue rivers and pass through the towns of Howard City and Sand Lake.

A trustee for The Friends of the White Pine Trail cites the trail from Big Rapids to Paris as the most beautiful section because of the Muskegon River, wooded hillsides, wildflowers and rural landscape you pass through. Paris is also home to the Homestead Grocery with its hand-dipped ice cream and the historic Paris Fish Hatchery and Paris Park, a great place for an extended break.

A trail as long as the White Pine has numerous options for enjoying this unique corridor. Those with mountain bikes or hybrid bicycles could load on their camping gear (or have someone sag for them) and ride from Cadillac to Grand Rapids camping along the

Cycling West Michigan

way, taking one to three days depending on how far you want to ride each day.

Because of its location, there are plans to connect the White Pine to other rail trails, urban routes and bike paths. In Kent County a proposed pedestrian/cycle bridge over West River Drive would link the trail to a planned network of trails to downtown Grand Rapids and beyond. For an update on what sections of the trail have been paved call the White Pine Trail State Park office ☎ (231) 832-0794.

Stage One (6.1 miles) This 26-mile round trip between Big Rapids and Reed City is an excellent ride to kick off the cycling season. The converted abandoned railroad corridor makes for a relatively straight trail with very gentle grades. There are no heart-pounding hills here to confront cyclists returning from a long winter layover. Most of all it's scenic.

The main staging area in Big Rapids is a train depot on the corner of Maple Street and M-20 that was built a month after the Grand Rapids & Indiana Railroad arrived in 1870. From the depot you head north and near *Mile 2* cross the Muskegon River on the 319-foot-long Whites Bridge. The railroad trestle is the longest of the 17 bridges the trail utilizes and provides an excellent vantage point to gaze up and down the river. Within a half mile from the Muskegon River you cross Dalziel Creek on a 30-foot long trestle.

The most scenic stretch of this stage is reached at *Mile 5.5.* A half mile before entering the small town of Paris, the trail sidles a bluff to put you right above the swirling currents of the Muskegon River and along side wooded hillsides that come alive in the spring with skunk cabbage and wildflowers. You then cross Paris Creek on a 59-foot long trestle and enter Paris.

Once in town you pass the Homestead Grocery that tries to entice you inside with a large sign announcing "Hand Dipped Ice Cream" and arrive at the historic Paris Fish Hatchery. Built in 1881, the facility is no longer a working hatchery but the ponds and raceways have been restored as a Mescota County park. There are toilets and picnic tables here for a break. Take time to check out the hatchery raceways that still hold trout during the summer.

Stage Two (6.9 miles) Beyond Paris it is another 6.9 miles through a rural landscape and woodlots to Reed City, currently the end of the paved portion. From Paris Park you immediately pass a farm pond with a classic white barn overlooking it. You are then

13 miles

Reed City

Pere Marquette Trail

US 10

Pecks Lake Rd.

190th Ave.

Hersey Rd.

Boyd Lake Rd.

131

Meceola Rd.

23 Mile Rd.

Paris Cr

Paris Fish Hatchery

6.1 miles

Paris

Northland Dr.

Muskegon River

Dalziel Cr

2 miles

N

Start 0.0
Finish 26 miles

Railroad Depot

Big Rapids

20

20

11.2 Cadillac

Tustin

4.6

Leroy

5.6

Ashton

7.2

Reed City

6.4

Paris

6.1

Big Rapids

9.1

Stanwood

6.3

Morley

6.8

Howard City

7.4

Sand Lake

5.3

Cedar Springs

131

7.4

Rockford

4.0

4.2 mi Belmont

Comstock Park

Grand Rapids

White Pine
Trail
State Park

rewarded with another view of the Muskegon River and Buckhorn Creek in a pleasant wooded setting.

Near *Mile 8* you cross 23 Mile Road and return to the rural landscape of rolling fields, red barns and dairy cows. Another scenic farm pond is passed just beyond 2 Mile Road and then the White Pine reaches the edge of Reed City at *Mile 12*. The rail-trail cuts through the heart of this town, passing such eateries as Dairy Depot and Osceola Inn.

The White Pine then arrives at the Pere Marquette Rail-Trail at a staging area where the original railroad tracks have been preserved in brickwork. If you want to extend the ride, head east on the Pere Marquette where a six-mile stretch was paved in 1999. The White Pine continues north, crosses the Hersey River and arrives at US-10, a very busy road. This is where the pavement ends. Beyond US-10 the trail returns to a loose cinder surface that makes it tough to ride on a road bike.

Stage Three (13 miles) Most riders backtrack to Big Rapids for a round trip of 26 miles. Hungry after the ride? There are numerous eating establishments in Big Rapids where cyclists are welcome. One quarter mile from the trail is Schuberg's Bar on Michigan Avenue, known throughout the state for its burgers. For middle-of-the road fare try Applebee's on Perry Street or Casey McNab's across from Ferris State University. For the vegetarian try Pepper's Cafe and Delicatessen, near Schubert's on Michigan Avenue.

Bicycle sales, service
Tour & Trail Cyclery, 204 Elm St., Big Rapids, (231) 796-2414.
McClain Cycle, 311 N. Mitchell St., Cadillac, (231) 775-6161.

Area events and festivals
September: Arts & Crafts Festival, Big Rapids.

Travel information
White Pine State Park headquarters, ☎ (231) 832-0794.
Friends of the White Pine Trail web site: *www.geocities.com/Yosemite/Trails/9394*.
Cadillac Visitors & Convention Bureau; ☎ (800) 225-2537, *www.cadillacmichigan.com*.
Mecosta County Visitors; ☎ (800) 833-6697, *www.mecosta.org*.

Central West Michigan

19 Nordhouse Dunes

Trip Card

Starting point: Ludington State Park
County: Mason
Distance: 55 miles
Shorter option: 16 miles
Terrain: flat, some rolling hills
Highlights: Ludington State Park, Lake Michigan, Nordhouse Dunes
Suggested riders: intermediate

M-116 is a friend to bicyclists. This road hugs the Lake Michigan shoreline and connects the town of Ludington to the Ludington State Park, the second largest state park in the Lower Peninsula. There are nicely paved shoulders on both sides, with signs designating the road as a bike route.

This stretch on M-116 is definitely one highlight of a 55-mile cycling route encompassing Ludington and part of the Manistee National Forest, located south of Manistee. Lake breezes, wide open sand dunes, a fabulous state park, the town of Ludington and even a designated wilderness area make this varied route enjoyable for cyclists. Beginners will find the flatness, spectacular scenery and length of the M-116 portion perfect as a shorter option route.

The 55-mile route begins at the state park and follows Lake Michigan before heading north out of Ludington, on inland roads. Then, almost as scenic as M-116, cyclists head west along the newly resurfaced Lake Michigan Road into the heart of the Manistee National Forest where it ends at the Lake Michigan Recreation Area on the edge of the Nordhouse Dunes, a federally designated wilderness. This 6-mile road is a cool, shaded avenue that cyclists will appreciate on any hot, sunny day. The lush foliage, blue sky above, and occasional deer that peer out from behind the trees will refresh and energize you. At the end of the road in the recreation area, there is a beach, campground, picnic area and two wooden stairways where you can stretch your legs with a climb to the observation platforms overlooking the Lake Michigan shoreline. The second half of the trip is a return to the state park and includes backtracking on both Lake Michigan Road and M-116.

It's easy to see why the Ludington State Park campground is full almost daily from late June through Labor Day. This 5,200-acre park includes 4.4 miles of Great Lakes shoreline, another four miles along Hamlin Lake and a series of spectacular dunes between them. There is also a short, paved bike route that follows Big Sable River, connecting to the park's Great Lakes Interpretive Center before merging onto M-116. If that wasn't enough physical activity for you, the park also features an 18-mile network of hiking trails, including a loop that winds through the dunes to the picturesque Big Point Sable Lighthouse.

Ludington is a year-round tourist destination but not the glamorous resort town (some would say suburb of Chicago) that Saugatuck is. Ludington is more a place for charter fishing, family-owned motels and cozy cottages on Hamlin Lake. There is a variety of shops and stores in downtown Ludington but our personal favorite, and that of most cyclists (or campers, runners, hikers, beachgoers...) is Ludington's House of Flavors (☎ 231-845-7360); it's the best place for rock-hard ice cream. There's nothing that hits the spot, or satisfies the sweet tooth more, than a hot fudge sundae after a long biking excursion on a warm, summer day.

A description of Ludington would not be complete without mentioning the Lake Michigan Car Ferry (☎ 800-841-4243) with rooms for 520 passengers, 120 autos and unlimited bicycles on the 410-foot, *S.S. Badger.* This service to Manitowoc, Wisconsin, was reinstated in 1992 and is a four-hour (well, most of the time, weather permitting) hassle-free cruise across the lake. Manitowoc is located north of Milwaukee and south of Door County, another popular destination for cyclists.

Stage One (8.2 miles) From the parking lot of the park's beachhouse (daily vehicle permit or annual pass required to enter the state park), head south on M-116, which is a flat road with wide shoulders and green and white bike route signs. Here the state's unique dune country will be on your left and Lake Michigan on the right. M-116 is literally an endless string of scenic spots along the Great Lake with access points from which to watch the sunset, listen to the waves or enjoy the sandy beach. The camper registration and information area is passed at Mile 2.4 and then you enter a wooded area briefly before taking a hard left to head north on Lakeshore Drive at *Mile 4*. This road has no shoulders, but is not heavily traveled. It twists and curves to follow Hamlin Lake for a stretch with the nicest views reached at *Mile 5.7* just before you pass Vacation Lane Resort.

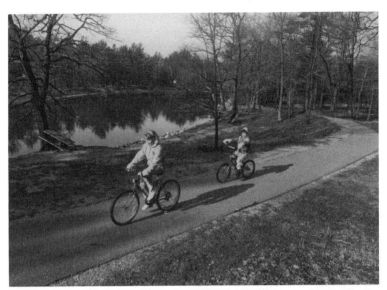

Young cyclists on the bike path in Ludington State Park.

The road curves to the right (east) and becomes Neal Street, passing more views of the lake and continuing to wind north until it turns into Stearns Road. The Sauble Resort (☎ 231-843-8497, housekeeping cottages) is passed at *Mile 6.2* and a quarter mile later you turn right (east) on Dewey Road; a narrow, tree-lined road with no shoulders. Turn left (north) on Jebavy Drive at *Mile 8.2* and Hamlin Grocery will be on the left and another market on the right. Time for a break, maybe??

Stage Two (17.2 miles) From Jebavy Drive, immediately turn right on Angling Road at *Mile 8.4* to head northeast through rows of trees and open farm country. When the road curves sharply to the right near *Mile 11* and heads due east, you'll be on Fountain Road, which has shoulders on both sides. Turn left (north) on Stiles Road at *Mile 13.2*, pass more rolling fields until the road ends at Town Line Road at *Mile 15.4*. Turn right (east) and then left in a half mile to continue north along Quarterline Road by traveling up a slight hill. A "Welcome to Grant Township" sign will greet you at *Mile 16* followed by a long, gradual uphill segment at *Mile 17.6*.

Now for one of the best parts of the tour! Turn left (west) on Lake Michigan Road at *Mile 19.5* and follow this nicely resurfaced road as it twists, turns and winds its way through the Manistee National Forest. The road ends at the Lake Michigan Recreation Area at *Mile 24.6*. There's a campground to your left and the beach straight ahead, reached in less than a mile. Definitely get off those bicycles and enjoy a extended break with a walk along the wooden stairway over the dunes and down the shores of Lake Michigan.

Energetic bikers can climb one of two sets of stairways to observation platforms on the top dunes. One stairway is nearby and leads to the trailhead into the Nordhouse Dunes Wilderness Area. The other is in the picnic area (tables, shelter, water and play equipment). This stairway is an aerobic 160 steps up but provides the best vantage point of the Lake Michigan shoreline.

Stage Three (23.8 miles) From Lake Michigan, backtrack the way you came, on Lake Michigan Road to Quarterline Road where at *Mile 31.4* you turn right (south). There are a couple of gradual uphills segments before you turn right (west) on Town Line Road at *Mile 35*. You continue to retrace the route by turning left (south) on Stiles Road at *Mile 35.4* and right (west) on Fountain Road at *Mile 37.5*. There are some gently rolling hills on this road before Fountain curves to your right at *Mile 39.8* and becomes Angling Road.

On the return, however, you turn left on Jebavy Drive at *Mile 42.4* and follow it south through both open farm country and residential areas as you get closer to Ludington. After a long uphill stretch, you finally reach civilization at *Mile 47* when just ahead of you appears a McDonald's restaurant! Here you turn right (west) on M-116 which is also the west end of US-10. ▲ *Caution: Even though this portion of the road is wide, it's the busiest in Ludington.*

As you cycle toward downtown Ludington, you'll pass several motels and a couple of bed & breakfast in century-old Victorian homes. In the downtown area, there are several restaurants, such as Subway, A&W and Old Hamlin Restaurant. At *Mile 49.2*, you reach Lake Michigan again and can take a break at the Ludington City Park which overlooks a beautiful stretch of beach and provides facilities such as restrooms, a source of water and picnic tables.

Stage Four (6.6 miles) From the City Park, head north on M-116 towards Ludington State Park. After a few blocks of sidewalks, you'll be on the designated bike route, with wide paved shoulders (yeah!). You'll cycle past the Cartier Park Campground and cross Lincoln River at *Mile 50.8*. A sign cautions you about sand drifting on the pavement but stay on course; the Lake Michigan scenery and cool breezes are definitely worth a little bit of blowing sand. This stretch is truly a cyclist's dream and before long you're back at the entrance to the state park at *Mile 55.8.*

Shorter Option (16 miles) From the Hamlin Dam in the Ludington State Park, cycle out of the park on bike paths to M- 116 and head south, closely hugging Lake Michigan. Pedal into Ludington to the City Park on Lake Michigan and then backtrack to the state park on M-116. This is a very popular bike outing for families staying at Ludington State Park.

Bicycle sales, service
Trailhead Bike Shop, 216 W. Ludington Avenue, Ludington; ☎ (231) 845-0545.

Area events and festivals
May: Carferry Festival, Ludington.
June: West Shore Art League Fine Arts Fair, Ludington.
July: Manistee National Forest Festival, Manistee; World of Arts & Crafts, Manistee.
August: Gold Coast Festival Arts & Crafts Fair, Ludington; West Michigan Fair, Ludington.

Travel information
Ludington Area Visitors Bureau; ☎ (800) 542-4600, *www.ludingtoncvb.com.*
Ludington State Park; ☎ (231) 843-8671.

20 Lake Cadillac Loop

Trip Card

Starting point: Mitchell State Park
County: Wexford
Distance: 44 miles
Shorter option: 7.2 miles
Terrain: flat route on shorter option, hilly west of Cadillac
Highlights: Lake Cadillac, Manistee National Forest, Mitchell State Park
Suggested riders: advanced on 44-mile route, beginners on shorter option

Contrary to what some people believe, no Cadillacs roll off any auto assembly lines in Cadillac! Many people associate Michigan with cars and automatically assume that Cadillacs are manufactured in Cadillac. Let me assure you they are not.

What this city of 10,000 does have is two large inland lakes with a state park between them. Ninety miles north of Grand Rapids and near the Manistee National Forest, Cadillac has plenty of recreational activities to enjoy including hiking, camping and cycling.

Departing at William Mitchell State Park, between Lake Cadillac and Lake Mitchell, cyclists can ride around Lake Cadillac on paved bike paths that are ideal for beginners. This lakeshore circuit is a flat route with lakeshore scenery and three parks, including a mile-long park near downtown Cadillac and the Kenwood Nature Center. Downtown Cadillac is a fun place to lock up the bicycles and go on a shopping outing, take in a concert or be part of any of a number of events held annually.

For more experienced cyclists, the longer route heads north and then west into the Manistee National Forest. This loop, with some long hills heading back toward Cadillac, offers a challenging workout through some beautiful forests. The road south of tiny Harrietta winds and twists through the forest while M-55 East, sometimes a busy highway, is more wide open with nicely paved shoulders.

There are not many places for food on this longer route so it's best to bring along a high energy snack or picnic lunch and then plan on more serious eating back at your state park camp site or at one of the many restaurants in Cadillac.

In May, you can combine cycling with another favorite Cadillac and Mesick area activity - morel mushroom hunting. The Harrietta State Fish Hatchery, located west of Harrietta, offers another option for a family activity while at the state park is the Carl Johnson Michigan Hunting and Fishing Interpretive Center.

Stage One (7.2 miles) From the day-use beach area and parking lot qt William Mitchell State Park, head south on M-115 which quickly merges into M-55. Here you'll find a paved a bike path on the left. In *Mile 0.7*, the road will curve left (east) past an "East M-55" sign. At this point, the designated bike route is on wide, paved shoulders that hug the lake. There are many residential homes along Lake Cadillac while South Shore Motel, a small establishment with 15 rooms, is on your left. The road curves sharply to the right at *Mile 3* (now called Granite Street), and takes you a through a residential section. At this point the bike path gives way to sidewalks. Cycle as close to the lake as possible and turn left on Laurel Street; take a right on Hector Street which merges into to Lake Street. Welcome to downtown Cadillac!

The downtown area offers an array of shopping and restaurants. The Sweet Shop (☎ 231-775-2201), on South Mitchell Street, is famous for its "Snowbird" candies. Made right on the premises, they're an addicting treat of white chocolate and pecan pieces - a natural for cyclists. For more of a fine dining experience, visitors will enjoy Hermann's European Cafe and Chef's Deli (☎ 231-775-9563), located in a century-old building on North Mitchell Street. It's a place known for its European atmosphere and delicious desserts. There's also an inn at Hermann's with rooms and suites. Room rates include an extensive continental breakfast.

Access to Lake Cadillac and a nice picnic and playground area is at *Mile 4* where you'll also find restrooms and a source of drinking water. At this point, the bike paths return and you turn left on Lake

Street within a quarter mile and then take another left (west) on Chestnut Street, closely following the north shore of Lake Cadillac. You'll cycle by Cadillac Middle School at *Mile 4.7* and remain on Chestnut Street until you veer left onto North Boulevard at *Mile 5.5.* This road winds down to the lakeshore again, with paved shoulders on both sides, reaching it at *Mile 6.* This is the most pleasant section of the lakeshore route with views of Lake Cadillac and stands of hardwoods across the road. You'll cycle through a nice section of trees and then reach the Kenwood Park Nature Area. Operated by the city of Cadillac, the area includes a community beach, hiking trails, restrooms, a source of drinking water and public boat launch. The Carl Johnson Museum is also located nearby.

You'll find bike paths on the right at *Mile 6.5* and then cross Clam Lake Channel which connects Lake Mitchell and Lake Cadillac. The canal was dug in 1873 after loggers grew tired of floating timber from one lake to the sawmills on the other through swampy Black River, a slow and laborious task not to mention the bugs they must have encountered. Today the channel is 48 ft. wide and used by recreational boaters, anglers and ducks looking for handouts from park visitors.

The campground at Mitchell State Park borders the south shore of the canal. At *Mile 7.3* you return to M-115.

Stage Two (16 miles) Turn right (north) at M-115. ⚠ *Caution: This can be a busy highway, in fact at the end of holiday weekends this can be the Indianapolis 500 with people rushing to get home.* But it has nicely paved shoulders on both sides of the road and you only stay on M-115 for three miles. You'll quickly pass a Day's Inn at *Mile 7.5* and then enter open country with sprinklings of birch trees before turning left (west) onto County Road 34 at *Mile 10.6.* Along this narrow road with gravel shoulders you'll cycle through a pleasant stand of trees that give way to scads of wildflowers. There are some rolling hills on this section, beginning at *Mile 13.4* and eventually you re-enter a heavily wooded section of the Manistee National Forest.

More wide open country returns when you swing sharply right (north) at *Mile 16.5* and at one point you can see far off into the distance. You are now on South County Road 23 and after passing cornfields you enter the town of Boon. Well, "town" might be stretching it, as Boon consists of little more than a Christmas tree farm, railroad tracks, several mobile homes and a gas station. A post office is passed at *Mile 17.4* and then the route becomes more interesting as it runs parallel with the Ann Arbor Railroad tracks for 6 miles to Harrietta. Along the way you climb a hill at *Mile 18*, pass more farmlands bordered by wildflowers that contrast nicely with the wooded areas that follow. At *Mile 23* you will come upon the sleepy town of Harrietta, where you'll find a small park and stately St. Edwards Catholic Church but few food options (bummer!).

Stage Three (7.7 miles) From Harrietta, backtrack south on Davis Avenue, also called 13-1/2 Mile Road. This road twists and turns through more wooded areas in the Manistee National Forest and then winds over a number of hills as you make your way back to M-55. Most of them are easy-to-pedal, rolling hills but you tackle a long one at *Mile 28.5*. At one point the road swings right (west) and becomes County Road No. 11 1/4 Mile Road before curving back east as County Road No. 13 near Caberfae Ski Resort.

The third stage ends with a fun hill and a couple of big curves. At *Mile 30.8* you arrive at a parking area to the east. This is a nice time to get off your bicycles and munch down on the refreshments you've packed along (you did, didn't you?).

Stage Four (13.2 miles) From the parking lot, head south on County Road No. 13 and within a quarter mile turn left (east) on M-55. This state highway can be busy, although you'll find narrow, paved shoulders here. More rolling hills are encountered along this stretch and probably the largest uphill pedal on this Cadillac route is tackled at *Mile 33*. After a few more hills, it's evident that civilization lies ahead as the number of homes and businesses increase. A Huron-Manistee National Forest ranger station and information facility is passed at *Mile 39*, where you'll find information and maps for hiking, canoeing and camping. At *Mile 43* you pass views of Lake Mitchell.

You'll cycle by Bill Oliver's Resort & Conference Center (motel, restaurant, golf course and bowling alley) and then enter the Cadillac city limits at *Mile 43.7*. It's now a short jaunt back to William Mitchell State Park, reached by turning left (north) on M-115. Time for a dip in the lake?

Lake St.

Hector St.

Granite St.

3 Miles

N

Chesnut St.

Sunnyside Dr.

Chesnut St.

LAKE
CADILLAC

55

5.5 Miles

North Blvd.

Sunnyside Dr.

KENWOOD PARK
NATURE
CENTER

North Blvd.

WILLIAM MITCHELL
STATE PARK

Start • 0 Miles
Finish • 7.2 Miles

Shorter option (7.2 miles) From William Mitchell State Park, turn left (east) on M-55. The road curves sharply to your right and becomes Granite Street. Turn left (north) on Laurel Street and then turn right on Hector Street to end up on Lake Street into downtown Cadillac. The return begins by turning left (west) on Chestnut Street. Stay to the left at the intersection with North Boulevard and this road will take you back to the entrance of William Mitchell State Park.

Bicycle sales, service
McLain Cycle Shop, 311 N. Mitchell St., Cadillac; ☎ (231) 775-6161.

Area attractions
Carl Johnson Fishing And Hunting Interpretive Center, Cadillac; ☎ (231) 779-1321.
Harrietta State Fish Hatchery, Harrietta.

Area events and festivals
May: Morel Mushroom Month, Mesick.
June: Lakefront Days, Cadillac.
July: Festival of the Arts, Cadillac; Fireworks over Lake Cadillac, Cadillac (July 4th).

Travel information
Cadillac Area Chamber of Commerce; ☎ (800) 22-LAKES or (231) 775-9776, *www.cadillacmichigan.com.*

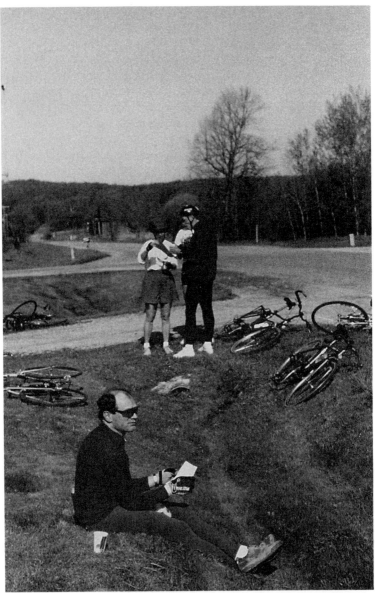

Cyclists take a well deserved rest during an organized bicycle tour in Northwest Michigan.

21 /// Crystal Lake ///

Trip Card

Starting Point: Beulah
County : Benzie
Distance: 24 miles
Shorter option: 8 miles
Terrain: flat, some hills at the end
of the longer loop
Highlights: Beulah, Gwen Frostic's
Studios
Suggested riders: intermediate

After cycling around Crystal Lake, it's easy to see why so many people make the area their second home. A stretch of the longer loop, on South Shore East and South Shore West, hugs the shoreline of Michigan's ninth largest lake and many feel one of the most beautiful. True to its name, Crystal Lake is an exceptionally clear body of water eight miles long and set at the foot of rolling hills and sand dunes off of the Lake Michigan shoreline.

For much of this route you are either passing scenic views of the water or summer homes that have been traditional escapes for generations of the same family. Unlike most modern condominiums that look like boxes stacked on top of each other, these cottages each display their own distinct style and character. From three-story mansions with numerous bay windows, to simple one-story homes for weekend getaways, you'll marvel at the variety of homes along this stretch.

The one thing that most do have in common are bicycles; in the garages, gracing front lawns or parked out front along a roadway that is predominantly flat with nice, paved shoulders on both sides. Cyclists of all ages can usually be found riding most summer afternoons.

Located just south of the Sleeping Bear Dunes National Lakeshore, Crystal Lake is definitely worth a day of cycling. A convenient place to begin your 24-mile shoreline circuit is Beulah, a picturesque town in a valley at the east end of the lake. Beulah is a great place to explore and enjoy a variety of eateries, and, of course, the shops and boutiques that flourish in many northern Michigan towns. The Cherry County Cycling Club recommends Northern Delights Bakery and Deli in Benzonia and pizza and beer at the Hungry Tummy in Beulah. There's also a variety of lodging, from the luxurious Brookside Inn in Beulah (☎ 616-882-9688), which offers rooms with Polynesian spas, to RV campgrounds, full service resorts and Chimney Corners (☎ 231-352-7522), your quintessential northwoods inn. We parked at the Cherry Hut (☎ 231-882-4431), a place for good food like their homemade cherry pie (with locally grown cherries) and great cinnamon bread.

From Beulah, the longer loop heads south into Benzonia, a slightly smaller town, then heads west along rustic River Road to another unique attraction, Gwen Frostic's Studios (☎ 231-882-5505). Frostic is a noted poet, publisher, artist and conservationist, who has lived in the area since the 1960's. Here she has created a personal wildlife sanctuary of 285 acres and a small publishing company where workers print her block designs onto cards, stationery, wall prints and books.

If you travel clockwise around Crystal Lake, there are a few hills and some turns in the beginning; then the route flattens out for the rest of the journey. The loop circles the lake at its west end on M-22, passing through Pilgrim, a tiny community near the Point Betsie Lighthouse on Lake Michigan. This popular lighthouse is every photographer and artist's dream at sundown on a clear evening.

For beginning cyclists, the shorter option begins in Beulah and goes counterclockwise, to avoid the immediate and somewhat intimidating hill coming out of Beulah into Benzonia. One friend of mine, returning to cycling after a long absence from the sport, easily handled four miles around the lake on the shorter route before heading back to enjoy a leisurely afternoon in Beulah.

Another way to add distance to the 24-mile loop is to cycle back to where you are staying. We stayed at the Platte River Campground, a marvelous facility operated by the Sleeping Bear Dunes

National Lakeshore. Cycling from this campground would add another 14 miles to the circuit around Crystal Lake. Renovated at a cost of more than $4 million, the National Park Service campground features pull-through modern sites along with rustic sites and even more secluded walk-in sites, especially designed for cyclists. Kids will have a fun time just cycling the campground's newly paved roads. The facility makes a fantastic home base when cycling in the Crystal Lake area or touring the popular Sleeping Bear National Lakeshore area.

By accident, we found a terrific spot, near the campground, where Lake Michigan Drive deadends. This is where the Platte River empties into Lake Michigan and families can spend an afternoon lazily floating down the river on tire tubes into the "big" lake. For a long float on the Platte there is Riverside Canoes (☎ 231-325-5622) at the corner of M-22 and Lake Michigan Road, where you can rent canoes, kayaks, tubes, rafts and paddleboards. Riverside Canoes also has a full-service general store with groceries, camping supplies and souvenirs. This is the perfect place to pick up a well-deserved Dove Bar after a bike ride or stock up on firewood for an evening campfire.

Stage One (3.4 miles) From Beulah head south on US-31. After a heart-pounding effort uphill, turn right (west) on River Road (also called Traverse Avenue), which is fairly narrow and has gravel shoulders. At *Mile 3.4* you reach Gwen Frostic Prints.

Her location on River Road is the ideal atmosphere for her artistic endeavors. The large galleries are housed in a building of native stone, glass and old wood where inside you'll find rough-cut beams, stone fireplaces and natural fountains. You'll be surrounded by Frostic's poetry books, woodblock prints and wildlife carvings by noted artists. Even more impressive is the publishing aspect of the gallery. From a balcony above, you can view 15 original Heidelberg presses clanking away as workers print a wide selection of cards, notepaper and wall prints. The gallery is open daily May through November and Monday through Saturday the rest of the year.

Stage Two (9.1 miles) From Gwen Frostic's head right (west) on River Road and you will cross the Betsie River at *Mile 5.3*. Turn right on Adams Road, a narrow road with no shoulders to quickly cross the Betsie River a second time. You're now in the Betsie River State Game Area; the rustic, even "wilderness-like" scenery makes for interesting cycling.

You turn left (west) on Casey at *Mile 7* and then jog to the right (east) on M-115 within a quarter mile where you encounter a long downhill. It ends with a panoramic view of Crystal Lake to the north just before you turn left (north) on Shorewood Drive at *Mile 7.6*. After climbing a long hill, the road twists and curves and climbs a few more times before you turn right (east) on Lobb at *Mile 9*. This road curves left and becomes South Shore East (also Country Road 702), well named as it hugs the Crystal Lake shoreline. Eventually it changes to South Shore West, a flat road with paved shoulders on both sides that winds past a variety of cottages and the sandy shoreline of the lake.

Stage Three (11.5 miles) From South Shore West, turn right on M-22, which is also called Pilgrim Highway. Soon you'll pass Point

Betsie Road, where you can detour for a short side trip to the lighthouse. The lighthouse is not open to the public but towers above a sandy beach in a very scenic stretch of Lake Michigan shoreline.

M-22 has wide shoulders as well as bike route signs along this stretch and beyond *Mile 17* of the tour it winds past Chimney Corners. At one time a downhill ski area, today Chimney Corners is a lakeside resort with 25 housekeeping cottages and one of the best restaurants in the county. Dinner is served only in single seatings Monday through Wednesday and double seatings Thursday through Saturday in a 1910 log lodge filled with antiques.

At the corner of M-22 and Crystal Drive, turn right (east) on Crystal Drive. This road is flat with paved shoulders, making it ideal for beginners. Crystal Drive follows the lakeshore until it merges into US-31. From here it's a short jaunt back to the starting point in Beulah. Time to enjoy a cherry dessert at the Cherry Hut.

Shorter Option (8 miles) From Beulah, head counterclockwise by pedalling north on US-31 to Crystal Drive and then turn left (west). Follow this flat road as far as you want, but within four miles you come to a nice spot to view the lake and rest a spell before backtracking to Beulah.

Area events and festivals
July: Fourth of July festivities, Frankfort and Beulah; Beulah Art Fair, Beulah.

August: Blueberry Festival, The Maples in Frankfort; Frankfort Art Fair; National Coho Festival, Honor.

Area attractions
Gwen Frostic Prints; ☎ (231) 882-5505.
Riverside Canoe Trips; ☎ (231) 325-5622.

Travel information
Benzie County Chamber of Commerce; ☎ (231) 882-5801 or (800) 882-5801, *www.benzie.org*.

Traverse City Area Convention & Visitors Bureau; ☎ (800) TRAVERS or (231) 947-1120, *www.tcvisitor.com*.

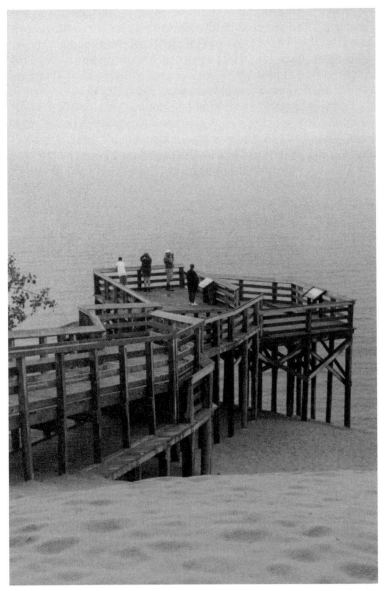

Pierce Stocking Drive features observation decks with stunning views of Lake Michigan and the Sleeping Bear Dunes.

22 Sleeping Bear Tour

Trip Card

Starting point: Pierce Stocking Drive
County: Leelanau
Distance: 36 miles
Shorter option: 19 miles
Terrain: very hilly in dune area,
flat to rolling in other areas
Highlights: Pierce Stocking Scenic
Drive, Dune Climb, Glen Lake, Glen Arbor
Suggested riders: advanced on longer loop,
beginners to intermediate on shorter option

Obviously cyclists were not left out when the National Park Service rehabilitated the 7.4-mile long Pierce Stocking Scenic Drive in the 1980s. How refreshing it is to see a wide, paved shoulder and a sign that says "Right Lane for Bicycles Only," after entering the road in the Sleeping Bear Dunes National Lakeshore.

This scenic drive is definitely the highlight of a 36-mile route that winds through the national lakeshore and around Glen Lake. The drive was named after Pierce Stocking, who spent his youth working as a lumberman in the area and later came up with the idea of a road to the top of the dunes so people could enjoy the incredible scenery from high above Lake Michigan. The road first opened to the public in 1967 and was called Sleeping Bear Dunes Park. After Stocking's death in 1976, the road was renamed in his honor. The loop is challenging because of the many long uphill climbs and exciting descents that follow. Cyclists must use the right side of the road and the route is recommended for experienced riders only. However, beginners can still enjoy driving through the dune area and then cycling the 19-mile shorter loop around Glen Lake.

Almost as scenic as Pierce Stocking Drive is Glen Lake, well-known for its sparkling blue waters. The lake has a unique shape, something of a warped hourglass. In the middle is the "narrows" where a bridge crosses between the two sections of the lake. The smaller half to the west is only 12 feet deep while the main part is 130 feet deep in places, although cyclists don't have to worry about that.

Another highlight of the route is Glen Arbor, a picturesque town with a variety of lodging choices from bed & breakfasts to the luxurious Homestead Resort (☎ 231-334-5000). There are also several unique shops such as the Totem Shop (☎ 231-334-3533) for Petoskey stones or Indian souvenirs, and Wildflowers (☎ 231-334-3232) for table centerpieces, perennials and wildflowers.

Stage One (7.4 miles) This is the Pierce Stocking Scenic Drive portion of the route, located three miles north of Emprie on M-109. At the beginning of the drive there is a parking area to leave the vehicle followed by a contact station where you can pick up an interpretive brochure that corresponds to numbered posts. Along with scenic overlooks, Pierce Stocking Scenic Drive includes a series of well-marked stops where you can learn about dune ecology and other nature topics. You are then faced with an immediate uphill segment, a good indication of the hills to come. There are shoulders on both sides of the road and soon you'll see a sign that says the right lane is for bicycles only (how nice!). Within the first mile you have a long downhill stretch that bottoms out at a covered bridge and a pull-over nearby so you can take time to enjoy the scenic spot.

More steep ascents and descents are followed by a scenic overview of Glen Lake near *Mile 2* and then Picnic Mountain. The day-use area is reached at *Mile 2.2* and includes tables, water, restrooms and access to Dune Overlook, the first of three spectacular viewing points of the surrounding dune country and Lake Michigan. All three overlooks have bike racks and the first two have short trails into the dunes. The trail at Dunes Overlook is Cottonwood, a 1.5-mile loop with an interpretive brochure available from a box at the trailhead.

Another tedious hill is encountered at *Mile 2.7* and is followed by a couple of sharp curves and hills, more hills, and even more hills! At *Mile 5.5* you reach the Lake Michigan Overlook where from 450 feet above Lake Michigan you have an excellent view of its shoreline and all the way to Platte Bay, 9 miles to the south, if the visibility is

Dune
Climb

Cottonwood
Trail

LAKE MICHIGAN

THE SLEEPING
BEAR

STEEP BLUFF

4
3 Dune
Overlook

5
Picnic Mountain
Picnic Area

6   7

2   M-109

Glen
Lake

8

1

10
9

Lake Michigan
Overlook

12

11

North Bar
Overlook & Picnic Area

Entrance
Parking

North
Bar
Lake

M-109

**Pierce Stocking
Scenic Drive**

To: Empire &
Visitor Center

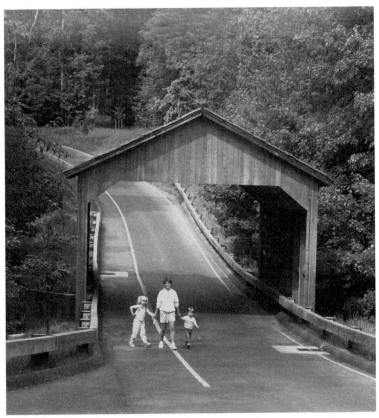

The covered bridge along Pierce Stocking Scenic Drive.

good. North Bar Overlook and Picnic Area with tables and restrooms is a short ride away, and from there Pierce Stocking Scenic Drive winds its way back to the entrance.

Stage Two (6.1 miles) From the entrance of Pierce Stocking Scenic Drive, turn left on M-109, a road with paved shoulders on both sides. You can see Glen Lake on the right and Lake Michigan sand dunes to your left at *Mile 8.2* and in a half mile will arrive at three National Park Service day-use areas, one almost immediately following the other. The first is a picnic area at the base of a dune on the left side of M-109, and the second on the same side of the road is the Dune Climb. This is, without question, the most popular stop in the Sleeping Bear Dunes as thousands of visitors annually make the steep climb up the wind-blown, 130-feet high dune. It's a slow trek up on foot, but the view on top is spectacular and the run back down wild. You'll also find restrooms here, a few tables, drinking water and a small store open during the summer. The Dune Climb is also a good alternate starting point for your ride, as it will keep non-cyclists happy while they wait for you. A little further north along M-109 at *Mile 10* is the Glen Lake Beach with picnic tables, water and a small sandy beach.

At *Mile 11*, just south of Glen Haven, M-109 turns sharply to the right (east). Continuing straight ahead is M-209 which makes an interesting detour. By following it you would quickly pass through the ghost town of Glen Haven and end up at the Sleeping Bear Point Maritime Museum, where the National Park Service has preserved a U.S. Life Saving Station that was built in 1901.

This tour, meanwhile, follows M-109 to the east and immediately passes the entrance to D.H. Day Campground at *Mile 11.5.* The 88-site, National Park Service campground is a rustic facility and a very popular one that doesn't reserve sites in advance. It also provides access to one of the most beautiful beaches in Michigan. Cycle to the log cabin shelter in the back of the campground where you will find a short foot path to Lake Michigan. Here the sand is sugar white, the water a shade of turquoise and the scenery stunning, with the Manitou islands on the distant horizon.

Continuing east on M-109, you enter Glen Arbor, two miles from the campground or *Mile 13* into the tour. Within this quaint town there's the Glen Arbor Bed & Breakfast and Cottages on your left and the Totem Shop, a unique gift shop on your right. There's also a mini-mart, restaurants and gas station, (need air in your tires?) on the left at *Mile 13.5.* If baking on the beach isn't your idea of the perfect extended break, then Glen Arbor is a nice alternative where you can walk around, do a little souvenir shopping or get a bite to eat.

Stage Three (15 miles) M-109 ends in Glen Arbor and you continue north on M-22 to quickly pass the Homestead Resort at *Mile 15.* Billing itself as America's Freshwater Resort, the Homestead has two restaurants, condominiums that are rented out year round, its own private beach and complete ski facilities (both downhill and Nordic). It also has prices to reflect all this. On this longer loop, you continue north then east of Glen Lake on M-22 as the road winds through rolling hills, and past picturesque farms. At *Mile 20.2* you pass Bass Lake and then at *Mile 21* turn right (south) on County Road 669. This road is narrow, no shoulders, yet lightly travelled; you pedal past School Lake on the right within a half mile. There's no public access on the lake but you get a glimpse of the water here and there through the shoreline trees.

You move into rolling farm country and at *Mile 25.8* turn right (west) on County Road 616, another narrow road with no shoulders. You'll cycle through a residential section and then at *Mile 28.2* CR-616 begins winding its way towards Burdickville.

Stage Four (7.5 miles) Keep cycling on CR-616, which in Burdickville merges briefly with County Road 675. The Glen Lake Inn (fine food, cocktails) is on your right at *Mile 29.* CR-675 heads south, but the tour stays on CR-616 which winds along the south side of Glen Lake. At *Mile 34* you arrive at the narrows, where M-22 cuts

❀❀❀❀❀❀❀❀❀❀❀❀❀❀❀❀❀❀❀❀❀

Beachcombing For Shipwrecks

The Manitou Passage between the Manitou Islands and the mainland shoreline around Sleeping Bear Point was a graveyard for sailors in the 19th Century. Between 1835 and 1960 more than 50 ships sunk in these rough waters. Today the area and its artifacts are protected as the Manitou Passage State Underwater Preserve but you don't need scuba gear to enjoy the wrecks. The staff at Sleeping Bear Dunes National Lakeshore has put together a brochure entitled *Beachcombing For Shipwrecks* and says it's a great area to search for bits of shipwrecks.

Most shipwreck hunters begin at D.H. Day Campground or the Sleeping Bear Point Coast Guard Station and from there head northwest around Sleeping Bear Point. Most of the wrecks were driven by November gales into shallow water and then subsequently torn to pieces by waves and then ice.

Search the sandy shore for large timbers of white oak which are black when wet but white on the outside when they have a chance to dry out. You can also identify shipwreck pieces by the cast iron hardware; spikes, rods, bolts and even rings, that are often still attached to the timber.

Within the park brochure is a drawing to help you identify what part of the ship you stumbled across and has some tips of how to age it. Ships of the early 19th century had wooden pegs as well as iron pins while bolts and nuts usually indicate a later vessel.

You don't have to wander too far up the point to find a wreck. Within a quarter mile of the station is a large piece of the James McBride, a brig that sank in 1857, of which almost 60 feet of it has been exposed for the past few years.

❀❀❀❀❀❀❀❀❀❀❀❀❀❀❀❀❀❀❀❀❀

the lake in half. You'll find hand-dipped ice cream at The Narrows Motel & Dairy Bar (☎ 231-334-4141), where rooms and double dips makes for a profitable combination. From the "narrows," it's only 2.4 miles back to the starting point. Where CR-616 curves sharply to the right (north), keep cycling straight ahead on Welch Road to quickly return to the entrance of Pierce Stocking Scenic Drive.

Congratulations, you've completed a strenuous loop, made easier by the knowledge that you're in one of Michigan's most beloved areas. Time to meet up with your non-cycling family members who are at the Sleeping Bear Dune Climb or relaxing in camp.

Shorter Option (19 miles) Convenient starting points for this shorter option around Glen Lake are the entrance to Pierce Stocking Scenic Drive, Glen Arbor or the Glen Lake picnic area on M-109. From the entrance of Pierce Stocking Scenic Drive, turn left (north) on M-109. Keep cycling on M-109 after it makes a sharp right and heads east into Glen Arbor. Head north out of town on M-22, then turn right (east) on County Road 675. This road winds around Glen Lake and merges into County Road 616 at Burdickville. Stay on CR-616 as it passes the "narrows" and where it curves sharply to the right (north), keep cycling straight ahead on Welch Road to return to the entrance of Pierce Stocking Scenic Drive.

Area attractions
Sleeping Bear Dune Climb, M-109, Sleeping Bear Dunes National Lakeshore.

Sleeping Bear Point Maritime Museum, M-209, Sleeping Bear Dunes National Lakeshore.

National Park Service Visitor Center (displays, audio visual presentation, information), Empire.

Travel information
National Park Service; ☎ (231) 326-5134.

Traverse City Area Convention & Visitor's Bureau; ☎ (800) TRAVERS (reservations) or (800) 947-1120, *www.tcvisitor.com*.

Cherry Capital Cycling Club, P.O. Box 1807, Traverse City, MI, 49685-1807 (send $6 for foldout waterproof map with other suggested cycling routes for northwest Michigan.)

23 Lake Leelanau

Trip Card

Starting point: Leland
County: Leelanau
Distance: 15 miles
Shorter option: 8 miles
Terrain: flat
Highlights: Leland, Lake Leelanau
Suggested riders: beginners

Beginning cyclists seeking a short, flat route in the otherwise hilly northwest Michigan, won't have to look any further than the upper portion of Lake Leelanau. This delightful journey, beginning in Leland, offers a sampling of what the region is best known for: fruit markets, public beaches and Leland, one of northern Michigan's most delightful lakeside communities.

The most charming aspect of Leland is its nautical atmosphere. The village's trademark is a row of weathered dockside shacks along the Leland River that at one time housed commercial fishermen and today is a historical district known as "Fishtown." The commercial fishermen are gone but their buildings have been preserved and now house gift shops and restaurants, including The Bluebird, (☎ 231-256-9081) an eating establishment that's been around since 1927 and specializes in fresh fish and mesquite-broiled seafood. Adding to the maritime setting is the fact that the ferries to both North and South Manitou depart from the docks of Fishtown.

More shops and restaurants are found on Main Street in Leland, including the Early Bird restaurant, which has excellent food and is a favorite destination for Cherry Capital Cycling Club members.

An ideal two-day get-away would be to combine a cycle tour of

Lake Leelanau with a day trip to South Manitou Island, a part of Sleeping Bear Dunes National Lakeshore. You can get to this beautiful retreat via the Manitou Island Transit (☎ 231-256-9061), which offers daily trips throughout the summer. Once on the island visitors can enjoy an island tour, hike the trails and old farm roads, view a shipwreck (from land no less!) or climb 116 steps to the top of a lighthouse.

Still want more riding time after 15 miles of cycling? The roads around the lower part of Lake Leelanau make for an interesting 46-mile loop. The tour is not only longer but harder as you encounter many hills. Attractions on the lower portion of the lake include Monstrey's General Store (☎ 231-946-0018), a place for hand-made wooden toys and bike repair, and the tasting room of the Boskydel Vineyard (☎ 231-256-7272), one of the most beautiful wineries in the state.

Stage One (4 miles) From the heart of Leland, cycle north on M-22 to quickly escape the Izod-clad tourists strolling downtown. This portion of M-22 has gravel shoulders and within the first mile you climb one of the few hills along the loop. There are nice views of Lake Leelanau at *Mile 2* and then at *Mile 3.2* you turn right (south) on County Road 641. The road closely follows the lake as it twists and turns its way south to Lake Leelanau. At *Mile 4*, just after crossing Houdek Creek, you pass a lake access site. The facility also includes a picnic area overlooking the lake and a parking area, which could be an alternate starting point for your trip.

Stage Two (5.5 miles) From the picnic area, continue south on CR-641 to follow the Lake Leelanau shoreline. The road is flat as it passes views of the water and winds through stands of birch trees or young orchards on the surrounding hills. The county road swings more to a southeast direction near Warden's Point and you take a sharp curve to the left at *Mile 6.8* and another sharp left a mile later.

After a downhill segment passing more views of the lake and orchards, CR-641 makes a 90-degree turn to right (south) where Eagle Highway merges into it. At *Mile 9* you come to a stop sign at the intersection of CR-641 and M-204, where an arrow points toward the town of Lake Leelanau. Turn right (west) on M-204. The Leelanau County Chamber of Commerce is passed on the right at *Mile 9.5* in Lake Leelanau, a scenic and untouristy (unlike Leland) town that straddles the two halves of its namesake lake.

3.2 Miles

LAKE MICHIGAN

22

22

Alpers Rd.

641

Short loop · 8 Miles
Start · 0 Miles
Finish · 15 Miles

LELAND

Horn Rd.

LAKE
LEELANAU

12.6 Miles

204

Popp Rd.

22

LAKE
LEELANAU

9.5 Miles

A cyclist takes a break at an abandoned barn in Leelanau County.

For a delightful side trip, and to add another seven miles to this route, cycle south from the town of Lake Leelanau on County Road 641 to Boskydel Vineyard on Otto Road. Boskydel is the first bonded wine cellar on the peninsula and from its small parking lot you have a view of sloping vineyards leading down the hill right to the edge of Lake Leelanau. The surrounding scenery once prompted a *Chicago Tribune* wine critic to call Boskydel the most beautiful winery in the Midwest. The wine isn't bad either and in this tasting room they plop down a large wine glass, not some one-ounce plastic cup. The winery is open year-round from 1-6 p.m.

Stage Three (5.5 miles) M-204 is a wide road with nice, paved shoulders on both sides and is relatively flat. Occasionally during the summer you'll encounter heavy traffic on it. From Lake Leelanau, the road veers northwest until it ends at the junction with M-22 at *Mile*

12.6. Turn right (north) on M-22 and within a third of a mile the state highway will begin to wind along the edge of the lake. ⚠ *Caution: This portion of M-22 can also have a lot of traffic on it but is flat with wide shoulders on both sides of the road.*

After *Mile 14*, you'll cycle into the heart of Leland and pass the dam in town. Try not to run over any fudgies.

Shorter Option (8 miles) Cycle north out of Leland on M-22 and turn right (south) on County Road 641 to a picnic area and lake access. The access site is reached within four miles and makes a nice place for lunch before backtracking to Leland.

Bicycle sales, service

Ralston Cycle, 750 E. Eighth St., Traverse City; ☎ (231) 941-7161.

Brick Wheels, 736 E. 8th St., Traverse City; ☎ (231) 947-4274.

McLain Cycle, 2786 Garfield Rd. S, Traverse City; ☎ (231) 941-8855.

Grand Traverse Cycle, 3337 S. Airport Rd., Traverse City; ☎ (231) 941-4868.

Area events and festivals

July: Leland Wine & Food Festival, Leland; National Cherry Festival, Traverse City; Leland Art on the Lawn, Leland.

August: Suttons Bay Art Festival, Suttons Bay; Leelanau Peninsula Wine Festival.

September: Leelanau Harvest Bike Tour.

October: October Festival, Northport; Fall Festival, Suttons Bay.

Travel information

Traverse City Area Convention & Visitors Bureau; ☎ (800) TRAVERS (reservations) or (800) 940-1120, *www.tcvisitor.com*.

Cherry Capital Cycling Club, P.O. Box 1807, Traverse City, MI 49685-1807; ☎ (231) 941-BIKE (send $6 for foldout, waterproof map with other suggested cycling routes for northwest Michigan.)

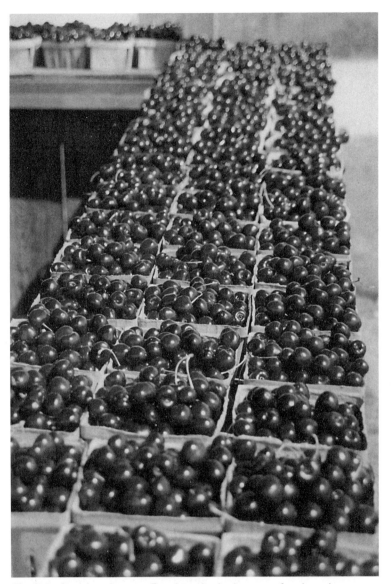

Fruit-laden Leelanau Peninsula is known for its cherry orchards, farm markets and nine vineyards, of which two are stops along this Suttons Bay tour.

24 //// Suttons Bay ////

Trip Card

Starting point: Suttons Bay
County: Leelanau
Distance: 27.5 miles
Shorter Option: 19 miles
Terrain: some rolling hills
Highlights: downtown Suttons Bay,
Suttons Point, Suttons Bay, wineries
Suggested riders: intermediate

This ride, beginning and ending in Suttons Bay, is another one adapted from the Cherry Capital Cycling Club's foldout map of routes in northwest Michigan and can be easily combined with other cycling tours in the area. The route travels from Suttons Bay south along the bay before heading east toward Lake Leelanau, another popular area for tourists and summer residents. The ride includes possible stops at two of nine wineries in the fruit-laden Leelanau County. Both Mawby Vineyards and Boskydel Vineyards make for an enjoyable break on this 27-mile route. Bicycling and wine anyone?

The route can also be easily combined with other cycling tours in the area. From Suttons Bay the Leelanau Trail extends 15 miles to Traverse City. Additional mileage can also be added by combining this route with the Lake Leelanau tour (see page 157). The shorter 19-mile loop is a good way to put on some quick mileage if other members of your group or family are too busy shopping, eating or strolling the boardwalks to ride.

Stage One (15.7 miles) Park in the business district of Suttons Bay near the Village Grocer. Head south on M-22 for a third of a mile and then continue on South Shore Road to skirt Suttons Bay. When the road swings northeast it becomes Stony Point Road and passes small beaches and homes. There are no shoulders here but the Stony Point Road is lightly traveled. The road twists and curves before you reach Vic Sternel Park at *Mile 3.7.* This small park has toilets, picnic tables and nice view of the bay from a rocky beach. Beyond the park Stony Point Road becomes North Nanagosa Trail and at *Mile 5.8* ends at Stony Point where the West Arm of the Grand Traverse Bay meets Suttons Bay.

Backtrack south on North Nanagosa Trail to Norris Road at *Mile 7.3.* Turn left on Norris Road and then within a third of a mile left again (south) on Donny Brook Road. This stretch of road has some nice size hills through rolling cherry orchards including the Stony Point Orchard. Turn right on McCallister Road (also labeled Town Line Road) and then left (south) on Lees Point Road at *Mile 10.2.* Here you cycle past some long sandy beaches and a resort area before you reach M-22 at *Mile 13.5.*

Turn left (south) on M-22. ⚠ *Caution: The state highway is a busy thoroughfare in the summer.* But you follow it for only a third of a mile before turning right (west) on Fort Road at *Mile 13.8.* To reach the L. Mawby Vineyard turn left (south) on County Road 633 (also labeled Elm Valley Road) to reach the winery at *Mile 15.7* on the east side of the road. L. Mawby Vineyards (☎ 231-271-3522) is at 4519 Elm Valley Road and open 1-6 p.m. Thursday through Sunday from May through October. This small winery situated on picturesque rolling hills produces table and sparkling wines on 12 acres. Winemaker Larry Mawby produces wines that are primarily dry, full-bodied and barrel-fermented.

Stage Two (4.3 miles) Backtrack north on Elm Valley Road and cross Fort Road at *Mile 16.2* before turning left (west) on Otto Road. This is a nice stretch of road for cycling with its rolling hills and orchards as you head toward Lake Leelanau. Otto Road jogs sharply to your right and then left before going up a large hill. You turn north on Maple Valley Road briefly at *Mile 19,* then left (west) within a half mile to continue on Otto Road.

Otto Road makes a lot of twists and turns as you catch glimpses of the blue waters of Lake Leelanau straight ahead. There's a sharp downhill with orchards and water ahead before you reach the Boskydel Vineyards (☎ 231-256-7272) at 7501 East Otto Road. Located on a side of a hill with a panoramic view of the lake, this small winery is reached at *Mile 20* and is open daily from 1-6 p.m. This

23.3 miles

3.7 miles

Stony Point

Norris

Finish 27.5 miles
Start 0.0

Suttons
Bay

Herman Rd.

Stony Point Rd.

Donny Brook Rd.

Smith Rd.

Norvick Rd.

Kohler Rd.

Pine View Rd

20 miles

Town Line

10.2 miles

Lee Point Rd.

Boskydel
Vineyard

Lawrence Rd.

Revolt Rd.

22

Maple Valley Rd.

Otto Rd.

N

Described Route

15.2 miles

Fort Rd

Lee Point

15.7 miles

L Mawby
Vineyard

winery specializes in varieties such as Vignoles, Soleil Blanc and De Chaunac from grapes that are French-American hybrids grown on 25 acres here. Boskydel is nice place for an extended break to take in the vistas and learn some about Michigan winemaking.

Stage Three (7.5 miles) Continue west on Otto Road before turning right (north) on Lake Leelanau Road (also labeled County Road 641) at *Mile 20.3*. The road here has gravel shoulders and makes a long uphill curving to your left before becoming a straight-away where you can pick up speed. You reach another flat section at *Mile 21.8* after a series of hills and then pass a farm market. Turn right on M-204 at *Mile 23.3*, which can be a busy corner. Head northeast on M-204 where there are partially paved shoulders. There are some fast stretches on this road as you pass Horn Road and County Road 637 and more fruit orchards.

Near the Suttons Bay City Limits sign at *Mile 27* there's a long downhill to enjoy. From there turn right on St. Joseph's Avenue to reach your starting point in the heart of the business district in Suttons Bay at *Mile 27.5*. Time to find the rest of your group, grab a snack at the Village Grocer or make other plans for dinner at the numerous eating options in the region.

Shorter Option (19 miles) To shorten this ride to 19 miles, turn right on County Road 633 at *Mile 15.2* and head due north on this road to return to Suttons Bay. Once in town you turn right on Broadway Street to reach the starting point.

Bicycle sales, service

Brick Wheels, 430 W. 14th Street, Traverse City; ☎ (231) 947-4274.

Ralston Cycle, 750 E. Eighth Street, Traverse City; ☎ (231) 941-7161.

McClain Cycle, 2786 Garfield, Traverse City; ☎ (231) 941-8855.

Grand Traverse Cycle, 3399 Veterans Drive, Traverse City; ☎(231) 941-4868.

Area events, festivals

June: Great Lakes Tall Ship Festival, Traverse City.
July: Cherry Festival, Outdoor Art Fair, Traverse City.

Travel information

Traverse City Convention & Visitors Bureau, ☎ (800) TRAVERS (reservations) or (800) 940-1120, *www.tcvisitor.com*.

Traverse City Area Chamber of Commerce; ☎ (231) 947-5075. Cherry Capitol Cycling Club, P.O. Box 1807, Traverse City, MI 49685-1807; ☎ (231) 941-BIKE.

25 T.A.R.T.

Trip Card

Starting point: Bunker Hill Road in Acme
County: Grand Traverse
Distance: 28 miles round-trip
Terrain: flat
Highlights: views of bay, downtown
Traverse City
Suggested riders: beginners

Traverse City holds a special attraction for those of us who live in downstate Michigan and the Traverse Area Recreational Trail, better known as TART, is the perfect way to enjoy this city. The 8.6-mile paved trail skirts the east and west bays of Grand Traverse Bay, and serves as a backdoor to the many business along the route. This rail-trail is unique because a portion of it parallels the still active Tuscola and Saginaw Bay Railroad. The path uses the railroad right-a-way and a fence separates bikers from trains.

The scenery along the TART, including sweeping views of both bays, is excellent. But the trail also provides motorless access to Traverse City State Park, numerous hotels and restaurants and even a zoo. Many businesses have tapped into this steady flow of two-wheel customers passing their backdoor. The Traverse Bay Woolen Company has a welcome sign and bench on the trail, Burger King has installed an outdoor eating area and a bicycle rack and Bayview Inn Cafe maintains a large thermos of water.

TART doesn't have the mileage for cyclists in serious training but is ideal for people who just want to get out, get a little exercise and enjoy those mild northern Michigan summers. Plans call for connecting TART with the Leelanau Trail a half mile away. Presently four miles of the Leelanau Trail is paved but eventually the two trails will be connected and surfaced to provide an excellent 25-mile point-to-point option from Acme to Suttons Bay.

Stage One (8.6 miles) The east end of TART is south of the M-72 and US-31 intersection. Turn south on Bunker Hill Road from US-31 and you'll quickly reach the posted trailhead. TART heads southwest and just before *Mile 1* begins sidling Five Mile Road. There are many views of East Grand Traverse Bay and US-31 below you before TART crosses railroad tracks at *Mile 1.3.*

You'll cross two wooden bridges and enjoy more views of the bay, then pass a Burger King at *Mile 1.6,* one of many eating choices along the way. The trail crosses another wooden bridge in a small wooded tract before skirting the back of more businesses including the Pebblebrook Fun Farm on the east side of Four Mile Road and an amusement park and Dairy Queen on the west side.

Within a mile you enter a scenic wooded and wetland section along the trail. To the north is the backside of Traverse City State Park, to the south is Reffitt Nature Preserve and at *Mile 3.6* a long footbridge over a stream. TART then crosses Three Mile Road and skirts Parsons Road. ⚠ *Caution: Both roads experience heavy traffic.* You'll cycle by the Cherry Capital Airport near *Mile 4.* Cross Hastings Street at *Mile 5.2* to stay on the trail. This is followed by a confusing section, but the green and white TART signs should keep you on track. You follow the paved shoulder of the roads for eight blocks rather than a separate bike path. Eventually you pass near Ralston Cycle on the corner of East 8th Street and Barlow Street and then swing north along Railroad Avenue to cross Front Street across from the Holiday Inn. At *Mile 6.6* the trail passes under the US-31 bridge and then crosses the Boardman River. Look for anglers here fishing for trout.

West of the Boardman River, TART skirts the West Grand Traverse Bay past some of the finest beaches in the area. At *Mile 7.2* the Clinch Park Zoo is passed followed by the Duncan L. Clinch Marina on the opposite side of the buffalos, bears and bald eagles. There is parking near the marina which could be used as an alternate spot to pick up the trail. Beyond the marina make a right to connect back to the trail near the Cherry Festival office. TART skirts the beaches in West End Park and then crosses M-72 and approaches the busy M-72 and M-22 intersection. ⚠ *Use caution at this intersection.* The western trailhead is reached at *Mile 8.6*, near Tom's Market, another option for parking.

72

Carter Rd.

8.6 miles

Leelanau Trail

Front St.

Cherry
Bend Rd.

31

22

West Bay

Boardman River

6.6 miles

Barlow St.

Garfield Rd.

8th St.

Parsons Rd.

TART

37

3 Mile Rd.

3.6 miles

Traverse City
State Park

East Bay

4 Mile Rd.

5 Mile Rd.

Start 0.0
Finish 28 miles

Bunker
Hill Rd.

72

31

Traverse Area Recreation Trail

Cyclists enjoy one of the historical markers found along the TART.

Stage Two (5.5 miles) To continue onto the Leelanau Trail cross M-72 and stay on the west side of M-22. There's a sidewalk here you can follow until you reach Carter Road. Turn left on Carter Road and follow it through a residential area to the start of the Leelanau Trail on the right. The trail begins with 75 yards of gravel before becoming an asphalt surface.

Currently five miles of the trail is paved. The asphalt ends just beyond the intersection between County Road 633 and County Road 614 but there are plans to pave more once funds are available.

On this five-mile section you'll cycle through some wooded areas as well as pass some homes and a small marshy area for viewing wildlife. Cedar Lake will be on your right. You'll cross a couple of different roads including Cherry Bend Road twice (also known as County Road 633) and Dalzell Road. Those with mountain bikes can continue on to Suttons Bay after the pavement ends at *Mile 14.*

Stage Three (14 miles) Backtrack your way to Acme, enjoying the sights, food stops and scenery along the way. Now it's time to make plans for dinner or gather wood for the evening's campfire.

Bicycle sales, service

Ralston Cycle, 750 E. Eighth St., Traverse City; ☎ (231) 941-7161.

Brick Wheels, 736 E. 8th St., Traverse City; ☎ (231) 947-4274.

McLain Cycle, 2786 Garfield Rd. N., Traverse City; ☎ (231) 941-8855.

Grand Traverse Cycle, 3337 S. Airport Rd W., Traverse City; ☎ (231) 941-4868.

Area events and festivals

June: Old Mission Art Fair, Traverse City.
July: National Cherry Festival, Traverse City.
August: Downtown Traverse City Art Fair.

Travel information

Traverse City Convention & Visitors Bureau; ☎ (800) TRAVERS (reservations), (800) 940-1120, *www.tcvisitor.com.*

Cherry Capital Cycling Club, P.O. box 1807, Traverse City, MI 49685-1807 (send $6 for foldout waterproof map with suggested cycling routes for northwest Michigan), ☎ (231) 941-BIKE.

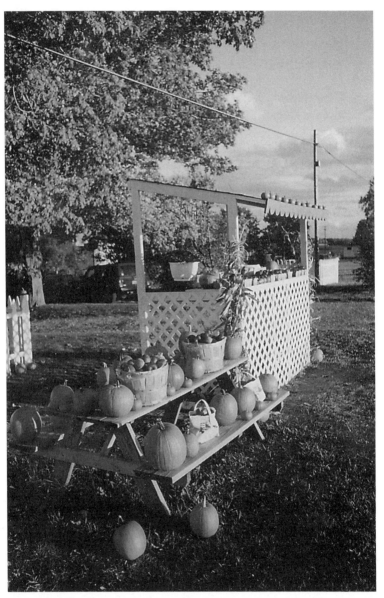

A pumpkin stand along the Old Mission Peninsula Tour to the tip of the arm that divides Grand Traverse Bay.

26 Old Mission Tour

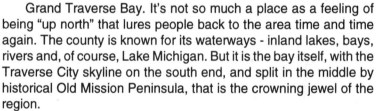

Trip Card

Starting point: Traverse City
County: Grand Traverse
Distance: 41 miles
Shorter option: 13 miles
Terrain: mostly flat
Highlights: cherry orchards, Grand Traverse Bay, Lighthouse Park
Suggested riders: intermediate on longer loop, beginners on shorter loop

Grand Traverse Bay. It's not so much a place as a feeling of being "up north" that lures people back to the area time and time again. The county is known for its waterways - inland lakes, bays, rivers and, of course, Lake Michigan. But it is the bay itself, with the Traverse City skyline on the south end, and split in the middle by historical Old Mission Peninsula, that is the crowning jewel of the region.

There is no better way to enjoy the bay, its scenic shoreline or the area's famous cherry harvest than by this 41-mile bike journey. You will traverse Old Mission Peninsula through one of highest density of cherry trees in the world; ripe, red, shiny cherries ready for eating if biking this route in July. Stunning blossoms will greet you in mid-May. You will travel a road that winds its way by the East Arm of the bay and then loops back along the West Arm, where across the water are the rolling hills of Leelanau Peninsula.

Vineyards, fruit markets, a restaurant with an outdoor patio, a tavern in historic Old Mission and finally a classic lighthouse in a pleasant park are all a part of the tour. Old Mission Peninsula is 18 miles long, while at its narrowest point this finger of land is less than a mile wide. This route is primarily flat, with a few hills thrown in to justify a hearty lunch. A beautiful stretch of the route is Bluff Road, which closely hugs the shore of the East Arm. There's no shortage of food choices on the peninsula. Area cyclists recommend the Old Mission Tavern (☎ 231-223-7280) for a wonderful selection of beer plus walls that double up as an art gallery.

This Old Mission Peninsula route is an excellent escape for anybody staying in Traverse City. Serving as the hub to northwest Michigan, Traverse City offers a plethora of lodging and lots of eateries. There is also a wide range of attractions and activities including para-sailing, sailing cruises, elaborate miniature golf courses, shopping, hot air balloon rides, orchard tours and a museum of automated musical instruments - plenty of pre-ride and post-ride options for everyone in your group.

Stage One (13.6 miles) Begin at Bryant Park, a small city park on the southwest end of the Old Mission Peninsula, just off M-37/US-31 in Traverse City. Turn left (north) on M-37 and right (east) on Eastern Avenue at *Mile 1.3*. Traverse City High School will be on your right and makes for another good starting point. Here you will find a separate bike path on the right. Turn left (north) on Birchwood (also called East Shore Road), a road with unpaved shoulders but beautiful views of the East Bay. At *Mile 4.4*, Birchwood (East Shore Road) deadends into M-37 where you turn right to continue north. M-37, which ends at the northern tip of the peninsula, has wide, paved shoulders at this point. ⚠ *Caution: M-37 can be a busy road at times, especially on the weekends in the summer and during autumn colors in early October.*

At *Mile 5.4*, you begin a slow but steady climb with a beautiful view of the bay to the right. Keep an eye out for Bluff Road where you turn right to depart M-37. Bluff Road is an exceptionally scenic section of the route that closely hugs the shoreline, offering panoramic views of the water and the other side of the East Arm. At *Mile 13.6* the road makes a sharp left before you turn right onto Smokey Hollow Road.

Stage Two (7.6 miles) Cycle north on Smokey Hollow Road where at *Mile 14.5* you'll encounter a long, steep climb past cherry orchards. A climb up another large hill ends with a gorgeous view of the placid bay below. Smokey Hollow ends at Old Mission Road at *Mile 17* where you turn right.

You've reached the historic Old Mission at *Mile 17.3*. Old

OLD MISSION
PENINSULA PARK

SHORT LOOP
Start • 0 Miles
Finish • 13 Miles

Smokey Hollow Rd.

Old Mission Rd.

25.8 Miles

17 Miles

Kroupa Rd.

Kroupa S. Rd.

37

Bluff Rd.

32 Miles

Peninsula Dr.

WEST ARM GRAND TRAVERSE BAY

EAST ARM GRAND TRAVERSE BAY

4.4 Miles

31

37

East Shore Rd.

72

BRYANT
PARK

LONG LOOP
Start • 0 Miles
Finish • 41 Miles

72

TRAVERSE CITY

175

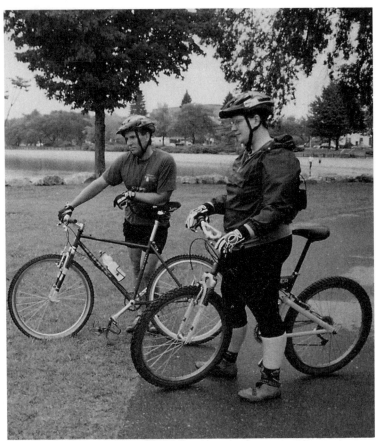

Cyclists follow the East Bay of Grand Traverse Bay during a tour of Old Mission Peninsula.

Mission was settled in 1839 when Rev. Peter Dougherty arrived from Mackinaw City; 12 years later a post office was established. Postmaster Stone received no pay and it is said that he kept the mail in an empty box nailed to his kitchen wall. When the letters arrived at Elk Rapids across the bay, smoke signals were sent up and somebody would paddle a canoe over to pick it up.

When the mission moved to the west side of the bay in 1852, Stone also took over the trading activities with local Indian tribes and built a store. Today, that store is Lardie's General Store, which for

82 years was managed by three generations of the Lardie family. Inside you'll find shelves and coolers stocked with refreshments or you can just take a break on the rambling wooden porch. Just down the street is a replica of the Old Mission Church that provides a better historical insight into the store and the area.

At *Mile 17.7* turn left (west) on Swaney Road. At *Mile 18.6*, turn right (north) back on M-37 (also called Center Road) and you'll reach the entrance to the Lighthouse Park at *Mile 20.4*. The Old Mission Lighthouse is almost another mile along the road. Built in 1870, the tower and adjoining lightkeeper's house sits just south of the 45th Parallel, the halfway point between the Equator and the North Pole. You'll find interpretive displays on this and the history of the lighthouse along with a beautiful beach, picnic tables, restrooms and hiking trails.

Stage Three (8.8 miles) After your break at the lighthouse, it's time to start the journey back. Head south on M-37 to pass a nice view of the West Arm at *Mile 22*. Cross back over Swaney Road at *Mile 23.8* to start a long uphill stretch. You pass the junction to Old Mission Road near *Mile 25* and then struggle up another long hill, reaching Old Mission Tavern at *Mile 25.8*. If a beer is not your pleasure at this point, you'll pass several sweet cherry stands that are usually selling fruit from early July to mid-August.

Turn right on Kroupa Road at *Mile 27*. This road is hilly, with no shoulders, and curves sharply to your left (south), where on many maps it becomes Kroupa Road South, although it wasn't actually marked in the real world. In the next three miles you encounter a sharp curve in each direction and then a gentle hill before turning left (east) onto Ne-ah-ta-wanta Road at *Mile 30*. Here you'll find an arrow pointing to Bowers Harbor.

Stage Four (11.5 miles) Ne-ah-ta-wanta Road twists to the south as it skirts Bowers Harbor, passing a public access site to the bay at *Mile 31.2*. Turn right at the stop sign by the Harbor Station. Bowers Harbor General Store will be passed shortly and then the Bowers Harbor Inn (☎ 231-223-4222). The restaurant is renowned throughout the region for its fine cuisine and steep prices.

The road continues to hug the West Arm for the rest of the route and becomes Peninsula Drive at *Mile 39.7*, where you will undoubtedly notice the wide shoulders on both sides. You're back in Traverse City at *Mile 40.8* and shortly after that Peninsula Drive merges into M-37. The state highway will curve to the right and at *Mile 41.5* you will be back at Bryant Park.

Shorter Option (13 miles) Begin on the northern portion of the Old Mission Peninsula. Cycle counter clockwise, beginning at Old Mission Tavern. Take Old Mission Road to Smokey Hollow Road then turn left (north) to Lardie's General Store in Old Mission village. Turn left (west) on Swaney Road and then make an immediate right (north) on M-37 which leads to the Lighthouse Park. Backtrack south on M-37 to the starting point at the tavern.

Bicycle sales, service

Ralston Cycle, 750 E. Eighth St., Traverse City; ☎ (231) 941-7161.

Brick Wheels, 736 E. 8th St., Traverse City; ☎ (231) 947-4274.

McLain Cycle, 2786 Garfield Rd. N., Traverse City; ☎ (231) 941-8855.

Grand Traverse Cycle, 3337 Airport Rd. W., Traverse City; ☎ (231) 941-4868.

Area events and festivals

June: Old Mission Art Fair, Traverse City.
July: National Cherry Festival, Traverse City.
August: Downtown Traverse City Art Fair.

Area attractions

Clinch Park Zoo; ☎ (231) 922-4904.
Grand Traverse Balloons; ☎ (231) 947-RIDE.
Music House; ☎ (231) 938-9300.
Tall Ship Malabar; ☎ (231) 941-2000.
Underwood Orchards & Country Store; ☎ (231) 947-8764.

Travel information

Traverse City Area Convention & Visitors Bureau, ☎ (800) TRAVERS (reservations) or (800) 940-1120, *www.tcvisitor.com.*

Traverse City Area Chamber of Commerce; (616) 947-5075.

Cherry Capital Cycling Club, P.O. Box 1807, Traverse City, MI 49685-1807 (send $6 for foldout waterproof map with suggested cycling routes for northwest Michigan), ☎ (231) 941-BIKE.

27 //Beethoven Amble//

Trip Card

Starting point: Interlochen
County: Grand Traverse, Benzie
Distance: 34 miles
Shorter option: 12 miles
Terrain: flat on shorter loop, rolling to medium hills on the longer loop
Highlights: Interlochen State Park, Interlochen Center for the Arts, Green Lake
Suggested riders: beginners on the shorter loop, intermediate cyclists on the longer route

Imagine camping in a state park with sounds of a string quartet, a jazz ensemble, classical music or a little blues floating through the air...followed by the sounds of applause ringing through Michigan's north woods. These are all possibilities when visiting Interlochen State Park, located next to the world-renowned Interlochen Center for the Arts.

Situated on a 1,200-acre campus, the Interlochen Center for the Arts is the umbrella organization for the Interlochen Arts Academy, the Interlochen Arts Camp and Interlochen Public Radio. The center is 16 miles southwest of Traverse City and over the years has built a reputation as an innovative center for teaching students music, theater, dance and the visual arts through a distinguished faculty and guest artists. More than 450 annual events take place in this culturally rich environment, including performances by the Oak Ridge Boys, Victor Borge, Linda Rondstadt, the Manhattan String Quartet and Peter, Paul and Mary, among other famous entertainers. Visitors are free to sit in on classroom lessons and rehearsals, and campus tours provide a historical perspective of the center and its 450 buildings.

Practically next door is Michigan's second oldest state park. Interlochen was established in 1917 to preserve a small tract of virgin white pine that was passed over by loggers and lumber barons in the 19th century. Today, the park encompasses 187 acres of land between Duck and Green lakes and includes a mile of shoreline, 490 campsites and a day-use area on Duck Lake with a wide sandy beach, picnic tables and a shelter.

Both the virgin pines and the famous music camp are highlights of a 34-mile bicycle route that begins at the state park and circles Green Lake. It then heads northwest to the small town of Lake Ann, before looping back to Interlochen via the west side of Long Lake. The 12-mile shorter option is a mostly flat route that circles Green Lake. Both rides traverse a beautiful area of hardwoods and pines, including an exceptionally scenic tract just inside Benzie County seen when you cycle across the Betsie River. It's one of those spots you would miss in a car, one of those quiet surprises that are especially rewarding to cyclists. On a perfect Sunday afternoon in September I was awestruck at the simplicity of the gently flowing river, the cottony, white clouds against an azure sky, and the leaves just starting to show their colors.

A great natural area, but what about food and shopping on this route? Local cyclists recommend Boone's Long Lake Inn on East Long Lake Drive for a "feast to remember". Near the state park, on the corner of US-31 and M-137, there's a strip of shops including Grandma's Kitchen which features homemade soup. There's also a bookstore and the Traverse Bay Woolen Company that offers items like wool sweaters and blankets, ski socks and winter jackets - a good place to do some early Christmas shopping! Dove Song is a flower and gift shop on M-137 with a unique selection of baskets, souvenirs and other locally produced items.

Stage One (5.4 miles) Keep in mind that Interlochen State Park, or any state park for that matter, requires a small vehicle fee or annual pass to enter it. From the parking lot in the park's day-use area on Duck Lake, cycle to the main entrance and turn left (south) on M-137. This road has wide, paved shoulders and winds through beautiful hardwoods and graceful, towering white pines. Green Lake Campground, the delightful rustic portion of Interlochen State Park, is passed within a half mile and then at *Mile 1.4* M-137 curves to the

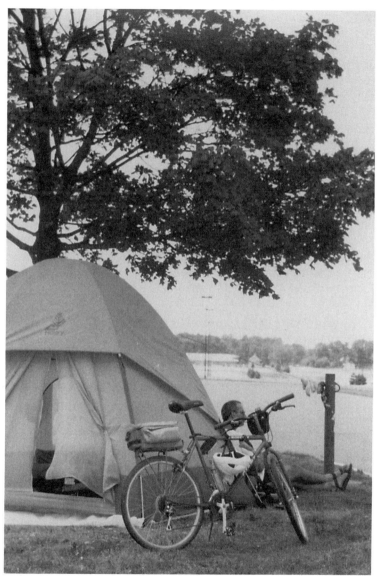

Interlochen State Park is a perfect destination for people who like to combine camping with cycling. This 34-mile tour begins and ends at the state park.

west and becomes Karlin Road. More curves and a gradual uphill stretch follow at *Mile 2.9*, where you will encounter gravel shoulders.

Eventually the road curves right into the small village of Karlin. Just before Karlin's blinking light at *Mile 4* you turn right on Betsie River Road and head northwest back towards Green Lake. The road curves immediately to the right through a stand of conifers followed by a large tract of mature hardwoods. After a few more twists and curves in the pavement, you reach a nice view of Green Lake at *Mile 5* and an even nicer spot overlooking the Betsie River at *Mile 5.4*. It's a great spot to pull your bicycle off the road and take a break, munch on a granola bar and feel the sun on your back.

Stage Two (11.2 miles) From the scenic overlook, cycle north and stay on Betsie River Road as it makes a 90-degree turn to the left (west) and one to the right (north) at *Mile 6.8*. Turn left (west) on Rhodes Road at *Mile 9* (also called County Road 665) to pass through more stands of hardwoods and pines. Eventually the road curves sharply right (north) at *Mile 10* and becomes a rather bumpy Lake Ann Road. You pass through a residential area at *Mile 10.3* and immediately follow up a steep hill. Cross US-31 at *Mile 12*. ⚠ *But be careful! These motorized tourists are in a hurry!* At this point, the route moves into open farm country where you will see a traditional white farmhouse with a stone foundation and the classic, faded red barn at *Mile 12.5*.

The hilly portion of the ride is now encountered. Take a deep breath and begin pumping, especially at *Mile 14.7* where you'll encounter a long uphill stretch before you reach the Lake Ann village limits at *Mile 16.3*. This is another beautiful part of the route as shimmering Lake Ann is to your left while the road curves sharply to your right at *Mile 16.6*. You'll find a couple of restaurants here (and thus restrooms).

Stage Three (17.7 miles) Turn right in the village of Lake Ann on Lake Ann Road and immediately climb a steep hill. You make a couple of curves to the left and head out of town at *Mile 17* along a road that is also labeled County Road 665. This is primarily a flat portion of the route until you make a sharp curve to the right (east) at *Mile 19.5* and merge into Cedar Run Road. You encounter rolling hills and more stands of pine as the road curves sharply left (north) and then immediately right at *Mile 20.5* before continuing east. Turn right (south) on Church Road at *Mile 23* which ends at the northern

72

23.1 Miles

Cedar Run

19 5 Miles

Church Rd.

N. Long Lake Rd.

LAKE ANN

LONG LAKE

W. Long Lake Rd.

S. Long Lake Rd.

Lake Ann Rd.

CO 137

Fewins Rd.

Honor Hwy.

31

Bendon Rd.

INTERLOCHEN

Rhodes Rd.

Start • 0 Miles
Finish • 34.3 Miles

INTERLOCHEN STATE PARK

8.9 Miles

GREEN LAKE

Youker Rd.

Karlin Rd.

Bestie River Rd.

N

KARLIN

Interlochen's Big Trees

Despite the lumbermen's Big Wheel near its entrance, Interlochen was one of the first state parks preserved because loggers had passed it over. The 200-acres of virgin white pine that somehow escaped the lumbermen's axes was established as Michigan's second unit in 1917 by the state legislature, which paid $60,000 for the land, the price of timber on it.

Today the old growth trees can be seen along the park's Pines Nature Trail. The mile-long loop begins on the south loop of the Duck Lake Campground and winds through towering white pine along with old growth red pines and scattered oak. The trail features 16 interpretive stops that correspond to an accompanying brochure available at the contact station.

tip of Long Lake. Here you turn right (to the west) on North Long Lake Road, a tree-lined avenue that hugs the shoreline of the lake.

Gilbert Park is reached at *Mile 25* and is a perfect place to enjoy a picnic or to just stretch out on the grass. You'll find picnic tables, volleyball courts and a source of drinking water. There is also parking here, making the park a good alternate starting point for this route. More rolling hills are encountered as you head south on West Long Lake Road which eventually swings away from the lakeshore into a mixture of open farm country and hardwood trees.

The road makes a sharp 90-degree curve at *Mile 26.4* as it heads back towards the water and within a mile it winds to a nice view of Long Lake. You pedal through a shady tunnel of trees as West Long Lake Road continues to wind along the lake before ending at South Long Lake Road at *Mile 29.7*. Turn right (west) on South Long Lake Road (nice paved shoulders on this stretch) and in a half mile you'll be curving south heading for the intersection with US-31 and M-137 at *Mile 32*.

The intersection is a major one and is lined with businesses, including a grocery store, bookstore and restaurants. Just a quarter mile south on M-137 is the Interlochen Motel, where the room rate in the summer includes continental breakfast. Shortly, you will enter the village of Interlochen and more food options at Cicero's Pizza and the Pinepointe Grocery Store. The main entrance to the Interlochen Center for the Arts campus is reached at *Mile 34* while immediately to your left is the entrance to the Interlochen State Park. At *Mile 34.3*, you'll be back in the parking lot - your starting point. Have any energy left? Within the state park is Pines Nature Trail, a mile-long loop that winds through towering white pine.

Shorter Option (12 miles) From the day-use parking lot of Interlochen State Park, cycle to the entrance and turn left (south) on M-137, which becomes Karlin Road. Turn right on Betsie River Road, which curves sharply to your left and then to your right as it heads north. Turn right (east) on Rhodes Road and journey to M-137. Head south on M-137 to return to the state park.

Bicycle sales, service
Ralston Cycle, 750 E. Eighth St., Traverse City; ☎ (231) 941-7161.

Brick Wheels, 736 E. 8th St., Traverse City; ☎ (231) 947-4274.

McLain Cycle, 2786 Garfield Rd. N., Traverse City; ☎ (231) 941-8855.

Grand Traverse Cycle, 3337 Airport Road W., Traverse City; ☎ (231) 941-4868.

Area events and festivals
June through August: Interlochen Arts Festival, Interlochen.

July: Interlochen Art Fair, Interlochen Center for the Arts; National Cherry Festival, Traverse City.

Area attractions
Interlochen Center for the Arts, Interlochen; (616) 276-9221.

Platte River Hatchery (4 miles west of Interlochen).

Travel information
Interlochen State Park, ☎ (231) 276-9511.

Traverse City Area Convention & Visitors Bureau; ☎ (800) TRAVERS (reservations) or (800) 940-1120, *www.tcvisitor.com.*

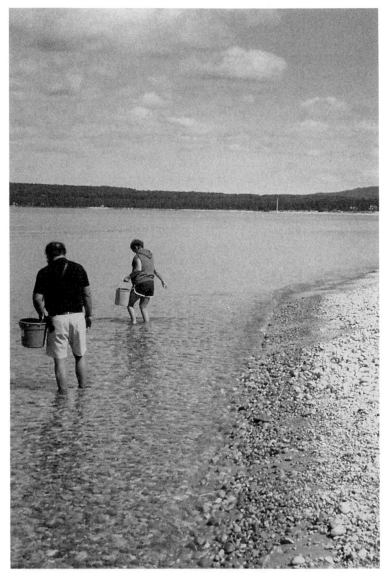

Petoskey stone hunters look for the state stone along the Lake Michigan shoreline. The state gem stone is a favorite with visitors in Northern Michigan.

28 Trip Around Torch

Trip Card

Starting point: Eastport
Counties: Antrim and Kalkaska
Distance: 47 miles
Shorter option: 4 to 8 miles
Terrain: mostly flat, some rolling hills
Highlights: Barnes County Park,
Grand Traverse Bay, Torch Lake,
Alden, fruit markets
Suggested riders: intermediate

When you look down while wading on the shores of Torch Lake, you see something unusual compared with many lakes further south; your feet! The water is crystal clear, allowing you to see any Petoskey stone lying on the lake's rocky bottom. Shaped like a torch, Torch Lake is 20 miles long, 2 miles wide and part of a chain of lakes that includes Elk Lake, Lake Bellaire and Intermediate Lake. But Torch is the crowning jewel of not only this chain but of northwest Michigan, a region, some would say, that is soaked with lakes, streams and shoreline. It's little wonder *National Geographic* once named this Antrim County body of water as one of the most beautiful lakes in the world!

Torch Lake is the highlight of this 47-mile route but so is Antrim County. The county is sandwiched between Grand Traverse County to the south and Charlevoix to the north and doesn't receive the travel writers' fanfare of either. What's missing here is the motel strips of Traverse City and the tourist-packed shopping areas of Petoskey. What you will find in Antrim County are small towns with historic main streets, acres of succulent cherry orchards and an almost never ending view of water.

Cycling West Michigan

This cycling trip around Torch Lake is an ideal way to see the countryside of Antrim County for those staying in a resort, campground or nearby motel. About half-way along the circuit, you pass through a town many people have never heard of, much less been to. Alden is a must stop for cyclists. It has small shops, an excellent restaurant and a historical depot being renovated into a local museum, all in a hillside downtown area that slopes gently to the shores of Torch Lake. I was immediately impressed by this picturesque town with its unpretentious air. It's a nice place to stretch your legs with a stroll by the lake or grab a bite to eat. Try the hamburgers at the Alden Bar & Grill, breakfast at the Country Kitchen (☎ 231-331-6777), the breakfast buffet at the Torch Riviera (☎ 231-322-4100).

Another well-kept secret is Barnes County Park, an Antrim County Park near Eastport at the northwest tip of Torch Lake. Although there's no fishing, boating facilities or hiking trails, the park has a pleasant campground and one of the most beautiful beaches around. This secluded beach on the Grand Traverse Bay has sugar-like sand that is bordered by towering pines, birches and other hardwoods.

Search the surf long enough and you might find a Petoskey stone, Michigan's state stone. A Petoskey stone is actually fossilized coral, recognized by its distinctive honeycomb pattern. When dry, the stones are hard to distinguish from many other rocks on the beach. But when wet the pattern is hard to miss. That's why you will see people standing in the surf and holding handfuls of rocks just under the surface of the lake. If that's too much work for you, any decent gift shop will have polished Petoskeys for sale.

This tour begins and ends at Barnes County Park. There is no fee to use the beach or the picnic facilities at this 120-acre park but there is a fee to camp here. Barnes has 60 sites, half modern and half rustic, with water, modern restrooms and showers. No reservations are accepted and in July through August the campground is usually filled on the weekends. Rarely is there a problem obtaining a site Sunday through Wednesday.

Stage One (11.6 miles) Starting from Barnes County Park off US-31 north of Elk Rapids, cycle clockwise around Torch Lake by first heading east on M-88. Cross the busy intersection at US-31 at *Mile 0.6* and immediately to the right you'll pass a public access site

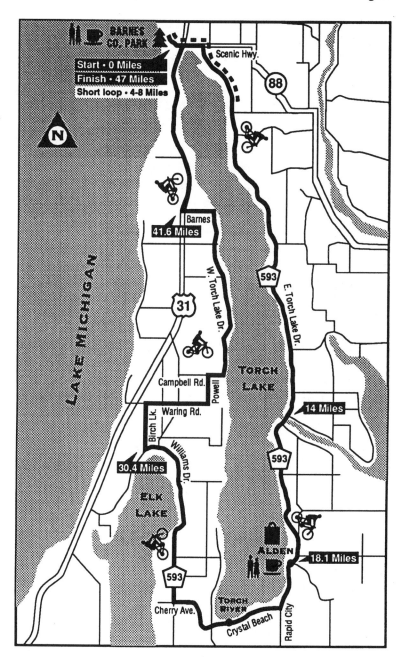

to the lake. Turn right on East Torch Lake Drive (also County Road 593) at just beyond *Mile 1*. The road immediately begins winding along the shoreline of Torch Lake as you head south. This road is not wide, but the traffic is normally light and the views of the water are excellent.

You enter a stand of hardwoods at *Mile 2*, followed by an open view of the lake and then encounter some rolling hills. If you need a break, browse through the flea market at *Mile 4.2* (you never know what kind of bargains you might find!). The route continues to wind south along the lake, passing through a heavily wooded area at *Mile 8* followed by a stretch of open farmland at *Mile 11.2*. Turn right (west) at the stop sign where there is an arrow pointing toward Alden at *Mile 11.6*. You'll still be on East Torch Lake Drive, although it's now called East Torch Lake Road.

Stage Two (7 miles) At 14 miles you enter the tiny hamlet of Clam River, where there are food possibilities, including Dockside Restaurant (☎ 231-377-7859). Dockside features a large outdoor deck overlooking where the Clam River empties into Torch Lake frontage that serves everything from hamburgers and pizza to antipasto salad and baby-back ribs. You'll cross Clam River and then immediately cycle by Thayer Lake at *Mile 14.8*. Cedar Shores Resort is passed at *Mile 15.4* and a half mile later there is another good view of Torch Lake.

You'll enjoy a long downhill stretch at *Mile 17* and then the road curves to the right. At *Mile 17.8* East Torch Lake Road curves to the right and becomes Alden Highway. This will take you into the town after a sharp right hand (west) curve at *Mile 18*. You reach the downtown area within a half mile and will find a variety of shops, an ice cream parlor, an old fashioned general store and Spencer Creek Landing, an excellent restaurant in a century-old Victorian house. It's pretty fancy (and expensive) but the couple that runs it also have a low-key cafe next door where spandex cycling shorts fit in better.

Stage Three (16.5 miles) Cycle south out of Alden. There's an uphill stretch at *Mile 19.2* where the road curves to the left and within a mile you'll be near the south end of Torch Lake. At this point the road has paved shoulders on both sides and you turn right (west) on Crystal Beach Road (still CR-593) at *Mile 20.4*. The south end of the lake is the border between Antrim and Kalkaska counties and you're actually pedalling in Kalkaska County. CR-593 curves to the

A young cyclist waits for the start of a bike tour. One of the most popular organized tours in northwest Michigan is around Torch Lake.

left at *Mile 20.7* past views of the lake and then you cycle through Torch River. There is a grocery store here and the Torch River Inn.

The road curves to the right at *Mile 23* and becomes Cherry Avenue (still CR-593) which begins with a long hill. More hills are encountered after you curve left at *Mile 24* and pass through the heart of Antrim County's cherry country. Cherry Avenue swings right to head due north at *Mile 26.7* and now features paved shoulders on both sides. You pass more cherry orchards, several large barns and even a glimpse of Elk Lake now and then. Eventually you swing to the left (west) and at *Mile 29* enter the sleepy village of Kewadin. You'll find a convenience store, the Oasis Bar and Grill and a few other small businesses.

Turn right (north) on Birch Lake Road at *Mile 30.4.* This road has gravel shoulders and is bumpy but has less traffic on it than Cairn Highway. Turn right on Winters Road at *Mile 31.6* and head east toward Torch Lake where it becomes Waring Road. You'll cross Cairn Highway (▲ *Caution: Watch for traffic*) at *Mile 32.7,* followed by a nice view to the east of orchards and then at *Mile 34* the road curves to the left (north) and becomes Powell Road. After climbing and then descending a long hill, you turn right on Campbell Road, a narrow road with no shoulders, at *Mile 34.7.* A couple more hills and you reach Torch Lake at *Mile 35* where you turn left (north) on West Torch Lake Drive; just up the road is a public access site to the lake.

You can take a well deserved break here or make a slight detour to visit one of Michigan's most unusual monuments. Instead of crossing Cairn Highway, head north on it and within a mile you'll come to the Cairn Monument. Dedicated in 1938, the monument honors Hugh Gray, who was instrumental in promoting Michigan tourism. It features a stone from every county of the state and sits on the 45th Parallel, the halfway point between the Equator and the North Pole. There's no tables or restrooms here but it's a scenic spot; from the top of a hill you're surrounded by cherry trees while on the horizon is a view of Lake Michigan. To return to the route, backtrack to Campbell Road and turn left (east) to West Torch Lake Drive.

Stage Four (12.5 miles) Cycle north on West Torch Lake Drive for some of the best views of the lake along the route. You'll pass through a stand of large pine at *Mile 38.6* that gives way to more views of this beautiful lake. You take on a short but steep hill at *Mile 41* and then the road curves sharply left (west) and on maps it becomes Barnes Road, although it wasn't marked. Turn right on US-31 at *Mile 41.6* for a five-mile stretch up the busy road. ▲ *Caution: US-31 has narrow shoulders on both sides so you must be careful!*

Travel through the Village of Torch Lake where at *Mile 44.5* you pass Schoolhouse Antiques, an antique store located in a refurbished one-room schoolhouse. Torch Lake Township Day Park is passed next and then the Torch Crest Party Store is on your left at *Mile 44.6.* But hold off on food! Turn left at Barnes Lake Park Road at *Mile 47* and there will be an ice cream store on the right. Go ahead and get the triple dip; you're only about a half mile from where you began in Barnes County Park. When cycling or driving into the park, watch out for the large speed bumps!

Shorter Option (4-8 miles) Cycle out of Barnes County Park , head east on M-88 and go clockwise around Torch Lake by heading east on M-88. Cross US-31 and then turn right on East Torch Lake Drive (also County Road 593). This road winds along the shoreline and is a scenic stretch. Pedal as far as you want to before turning around and backtracking to Barnes County Park.

Bicycle sales, service
Ralston Cycle, 750 E. Eighth St., Traverse City; ☎ (231) 941-7161.

Brick Wheels, 736 8th St., Traverse City; ☎ (231) 947-4274.

McLain Cycle, 2786 Garfield Rd. N., Traverse City; ☎ (231) 941-8855.

High Gear, 1187 N. US-31, Petoskey; ☎ (231) 347-6118.

Bicycle repair
Fitness Source & Cycle, 100 N. Division Rd., Petoskey; (231) 347-6877.

Area events and festivals
June: Art Fair, Elk Rapids.

July: R.A.T. (Ride Around Torch), Cherry Capital Cycling Club, Torch Lake; Venetian Festival, Charlevoix.

August: Harbor Days Festival (with bike races), Elk Rapids.

October: Apple Festival, Charlevoix.

Travel information
Elk Rapids Chamber of Commerce; ☎ (231) 264-8202.

Cherry Capital Cycling Club, P.O. Box 1807, Traverse City, MI 49685-1807; ☎ (231) 941-BIKE.

Hemingway's Horton Bay General Store, where the author idled away his youthful summers, is a popular stop along the Lake Charlevoix bicycle tour.

29 ///Hemingway Tour///

Trip Card

Starting point: Charlevoix
County: Charlevoix
Distance: 35 miles
Shorter option: 12 miles
Terrain: flat, some rolling hills
Highlights: Horton Bay General
Store, Boyne City, Avalanche Peak,
Ironton Ferry
Suggested riders: intermediate

Horton Bay, the town, was only five houses on
the main road between Boyne City and
Charlevoix. There was the general store and
post office with a high false front and maybe a
wagon hitched out in front...

Ernest Hemingway, from *"Up in Michigan"*

Charlevoix. Ah, beautiful Charlevoix. Even its name is inviting.
Charlevoix is a picturesque town, with multi-colored petunias lining
the streets. As you approach, all eyes are drawn to a canvas of
sailboats on tiny Round Lake, seemingly in the middle of the
downtown area.

But Round Lake is just a teaser to the larger Lake Charlevoix,
which makes an excellent 35-mile bicycling circuit if you bypass the
south arm via the Ironton Ferry. Charlevoix, a town of more than
3,000 residents (it probably triples during the summer), is a good
place to begin and end your bike ride. There are plenty of post-ride
options such as shopping, art galleries and festivals throughout the

vacation season. Non-cyclists in the group will be more than happy to wait here for the adventurous souls to complete their loop.

Pleasing terrain, wonderful scenery, many pleasant parks and a little bit of Hemingway history is what this challenging 35-mile circuit offers. Several of Ernest Hemingway's Nick Adams stories take place in settings from the area around Charlevoix and Walloon lakes while a description of Horton Bay General Store opens up his tale, "Up In Michigan." This two-story structure built in 1876 has a wide front porch, inviting visitors in to walk across its worn, wooden floors or idle away a summer afternoon as a young Hemingway often did. Inside is something of a shrine to its famous patron, with guns, old traps, mounted deer heads and numerous photos of Hemingway. It's still a general store, though, with ice cream, cold drinks and counter where the morning coffee drinkers gather.

The 49 residents of tiny Horton Bay don't seem to take themselves too seriously. Every Fourth of July the village hosts a wacky, tongue-in-cheek parade, which draws thousands of spectators. One parade featured Murphy Brown impersonators, the "Dan Quayle Spelling School" float, rock bands (instead of marching bands) on flatbed trailers, a parade viewing stand at the Horton Bay General Store, and llamas instead of horses.

A fun stopover on this journey around Lake Charlevoix is Ironton. To avoid cycling an additional 16 miles around the south arm of the lake, cyclists (and cars) can take passage on the Ironton Ferry for a five-minute ride across the arm. The historical ferry is beloved by the locals as it is no more than a barge on a cable and was once featured in the "Ripley's Believe It or Not" column. The ferry service dates back to 1876, and is operated on demand as operators can easily see when their service is needed. As a cyclist, it's fun to cruise ahead of the cars and not wait on a busy summer day - there's only room for four vehicles, but there is always room for another person on a bicycle.

The south shore of Lake Charlevoix is definitely easier and flatter. A shorter option for beginners is to cycle from Boyne City on the south shore of the lake as far as desired and then backtrack to Boyne City. From Boyne City to the Ironton Ferry is just over 11 miles, a pleasant journey that closely follows the lake.

In Charlevoix, you'll find a wide variety of lodging and eateries. There are moderate-priced motels, luxurious condominium suites

❀❀❀❀❀❀❀❀❀❀❀❀❀❀❀❀❀❀❀❀

In Search Of Ernest Hemingway

From infancy to the age of 22, Ernest Hemingway spent almost all his summers at his family's cottage on Walloon Lake and in Horton Bay. The Nobel Prize winner actually stayed at Eva Potter's rooming house at State and Woodland Streets in Petoskey to get away from his parents and to do some serious writing. He was also a frequent visitor to the Noggin Room located in the Perry Hotel.

In 1916, Hemingway returned to the area after a fishing trip, which formed the background to his classic short story, "The Battler." He also hung out at the Horton Bay General Store as a youth, fished Horton Creek for brook trout and in 1921 celebrated his first marriage to Hadley Richardson in Horton Bay's Congregational Church. Eventually the general store appeared in the opening of his short story "Up in Michigan,"

Hemingway buffs often tour the area to view artifacts and places that made their way into his writing and usually begin at Little Traverse Historical Museum (231-347-2620) on Dock St. in Petoskey's picturesque waterfront. Housed in the 1892 Chicago and West Michigan Railroad Depot, the museum's Hemingway collection is small but does contain photographs, other memorabilia, and some rare first-edition books that Hemingway autographed for his friend, Edwin Pailthrorp, whom he visited in Petoskey in 1947.

Horton Bay is the highlight of any literary tour but many Hemingway buffs continue following the Lake Charlevoix shoreline to Ferry Road on the south side. Right before reaching the South Arm of the lake, they turn north onto Sanderson Road to reach Hemingway Point. Originally owned by Hemingway's uncle, it's said that the young author once fled across the lake to the point to elude a conservation officer in Horton Bay.

❀❀❀❀❀❀❀❀❀❀❀❀❀❀❀❀❀❀❀❀

and six bed & breakfast establishments, including the Charlevoix Country Inn (☎ 231-547-5134) that was built in 1896 and overlooks Lake Michigan. For campers, there is Fisherman's Island State Park, five miles south of Charlevoix on US-31. The 2,678-acre park not only has some great beaches and good hunting for Petoskey stones but most popular are its 15 rustic sites right on the shoreline where your tent is only a few feet from the lapping waters of Lake Michigan.

On your spare day you might consider a day trip to Beaver Island, known as the "Emerald Isle" for its strong Irish heritage. An unspoiled paradise, the island is a haven for mountain bikers with plenty of gravel roads. Beaver Island has a lodge, hotels and camp sites available along with a couple of interesting museums, specialty shops and lighthouses. The Beaver Island Boat Company (☎ 231-547-2311) offers passenger and car ferry service to the island. Every day from mid-June through Labor day, visitors can leave for the island in the morning and return to Charlevoix that same day.

Stage One (10 miles) We started this route from the VFW Hall, located north of the business district of Charlevoix, although any place in Charlevoix will work as a good starting point. Cycle the route in a clockwise direction, heading north out of Charlevoix. From US-31, turn right on Boyne City Road within a half mile. This road has gravel shoulders and is hilly in places but lightly travelled. You encounter a long hill at *Mile 1.6* and then the road winds it way south passing good views of Lake Charlevoix at *Mile 6*. More twists and curves follow and at *Mile 8.6* you head downhill past a llama farm.

A "Welcome to Bay Township" sign can be seen at *Mile 9* and another hill is confronted before you enter Horton Bay, population 49! Horton Bay General Store will be to the left at *Mile 10* while nearby is the Red Fox Inn Tourist Room and Heartwell & Co. Bookstore. Horton Bay is a good place to get off those bicycles and have a look around where Hemingway used to hang out.

Stage Two (5.7 miles) From Horton Bay it's downhill, when Boyne City Road curves to the right at *Mile 10.4*. You'll find paved shoulders on both sides of the road at *Mile 14* and then arrive at the entrance of Young State Park. The 563-acre park features 240 modern campsites in three camping areas along with three miles of hiking trails and a wide sandy beach in its day-use area. This is an alternate place to begin the tour, but if you plan to camp here reserve

SHORT RIDE
Start • 0 Miles
Finish • 12 Miles

BOYNE CITY

14.1 Miles

Charlevoix-Boyne City

N

YOUNG STATE PARK

Lakeshore Rd.

HORTON BAY

WHITING COUNTY PARK

9.9 Miles

19.8 Miles

C-56

LAKE CHARLEVOIX

Ferry Rd.

Charlevoix

Boyne City

IRONTON

26.8 Miles

LONG RIDE
Start • 0 Miles
Finish • 35 Miles

66

CHARLEVOIX

a site in advance. The campground is filled almost daily from early July to mid-August. The park is also an excellent place for that snack or lunch you packed as there is a grassy picnic area overlooking the beach and a concessionaire store.

Boyne City limits is just down the road at *Mile 14.6*; after passing through a residential section the road curves sharply to the right into the downtown area at *Mile 15.4*. In town, the road is called Michigan Avenue and public restrooms will be passed to your right at *Mile 15.7*. Boyne City is a charming place on the lake with a distinct main street of shops, restaurants and lodging. For fine dining, try Stafford's One Water Street (☎ 231-582-3434), part of the Stafford chain or try The Depot for an overall good meal.

Stage Three (11 miles) From Boyne City, cycle on North Lake Street past Lake Charlevoix and the marina. Veterans Memorial Park is to the right at *Mile 16.6* where you'll find public restrooms nearby. Turn right on Main Street, which curves to the left and becomes Front Street still closely hugging the lakeshore. There's another public park to your right at *Mile 17* before bike paths appear on the right hand side of the road at *Mile 17.4*. The road becomes North Division Street again as it follows the lakeshore and then Lake Shore Drive.

A short but interesting side trip here is to ride to Avalanche Overlook Park for some of the best vistas in northwest Michigan. Just before Division Street turns into Lake Shore Road, turn left on Lake Street and then left on Ann Street. The park is a quarter mile at the end of Ann Street.

How steep is Avalanche Overlook? It's 473 steps and 11 rest benches to the top and was once a downhill ski slope. But from its lofty peak, you can see all of Boyne City, the length of Lake Charlevoix and the hills that surround it to the north. You can practically see this entire 35-mile bicycle tour.

Back on Lake Shore, there is not a lot of traffic, but the pavement can be a little rough before things smooth out at *Mile 18.5*. You'll cycle through the small village of Advance at *Mile 19.8*, where you'll find a grocery store on the corner and the road to East Jordan. Continue straight, following the lakeshore and soon a sign appears saying "Ironton Ferry is Open." Yeah!! As you look across the lake, you'll enjoy its hue of greenish blues, especially on a sunny day before a steep hill at *Mile 21.4* interrupts your day-dreaming. At

The Ironton Ferry carries cyclists across the South Arm.

Whiting County Park the road swings away from the lake and becomes Ferry Road. Shift gears, climb another hill, which curves to the right at *Mile 23*, pass a golf course and a scattering of homes and you'll be rewarded at *Mile 26.4* with a long downhill stretch. Ferry Road ends at the Ironton Ferry (how appropriate!) at *Mile 26.8*. Time to cruise ahead of any cars waiting there and pay your 50 cents for the short 5-minute ride on this unique cable-operated ferry.

Stage Four (7.9 miles) From the ferry landing, the road curves to the right and travels up a steep hill and northwest towards Charlevoix on M-66. M-66 features wide, paved shoulders on both sides and at *Mile 32* it deadends into US-31. Turn right on US-31 for a short jaunt back to Charlevoix.

Civilization in the form of fast food is now in view. McDonald's will be to your right, and Pizza Hut to your left at *Mile 32.4*. In downtown Charlevoix, US-31 narrows to two lanes of traffic (called Bridge Street here), causing a major bottleneck for summer tourists. Be careful as you cycle through this stretch and pay attention to the possibilities for post-ride options: fine dining, maybe an art fair, or perhaps a scenic cruise. Hungry? Try Tom's Mom's for huge cookies, soups and sandwiches. You'll be back to your starting point at the VFW Hall at *Mile 34.7.*

Shorter Option (12 miles) From Boyne City, head south following the lakeshore and then northwest along Lake Shore Drive. A little more than six miles, Whiting County Park is a perfect place to stop and rest before backtracking to your car.

Bicycle sales, service
Ace Hardware, 403 Bridge St., Charlevoix; ☎ (231) 547-4841.
High Gear, 1187 N. US-31, Petoskey; ☎ (231) 347-6118.
Fitness Source & Cycle, 100 N. Division Rd., Petoskey; ☎ (231) 347-6877.

Area events and festivals
May: Petunia Planting, Charlevoix.
July: Venetian Festival, Charlevoix; Craft Show, Charlevoix; Annual Home Tour, Charlevoix; Fourth of July parade, Horton Bay.
August: Waterfront Art Fair & Castle Farm Art Show, Charlevoix; Sidewalk sales, Charlevoix.
October: Apple Fest, Charlevoix.

Area attractions
Horton Bay General Store, Horton Bay; ☎ (231) 582-7827.
Ironton Ferry, Ironton; ☎ (231) 547-9036
Beaver Island Boat Co., Charlevoix; ☎ (231) 547-2311.
Pirate's Cove Adventure Golf, Petoskey; ☎ (231) 347-1123.

Travel information
Charlevoix Chamber of Commerce; ☎ (231) 547-2101.
Charlevoix Convention & Visitors Bureau; ☎ (800) 367-8557.
Boyne City Chamber of Commerce; ☎ (231) 582-6222.
Boyne Country Convention & Visitors Bureau; ☎ (800) 845-2828 or (231) 348-2755, *www.boynecountry.com.*

30 Tunnel of Trees

Trip Card

Starting point: Harbor Springs
County: Emmet
Distance: 38 miles
Shorter option: 18 miles
Terrain: hilly on M-119, flat to rolling on inland roads
Highlights: Harbor Springs, Legs Inn, M-119 Tunnel of Trees, Lake Michigan overlooks
Suggested riders: intermediate to advanced

National Geographic magazine once called M-119 one of the most beautiful drives in the country. Little wonder why. From Harbor Springs northward, the state highway follows the rugged Lake Michigan coastline but more times than not there is no view of the Great Lake whatsoever. The beauty of this narrow road is found in the trees shading the pavement, in the tunnels of trees you pass through and not the views you gaze upon.

Throughout this book, I've written about tunnels and canopies of trees. Indeed, Michigan is blessed with an abundance of species of hardwood trees that form canopies that people from other states drool over (well, not literally). But here we could affectionately call the Cross Village route the "mother of all tunnels of trees." M-119 is the longest, the most rolling, and the greenest of all tunnels. You get the picture.

Perched high above the Lake Michigan shoreline, M-119 provides tantalizing glimpses of the lake, but mostly it's the roadside lined with trees and the hills that wind, dip and curve, that provide bicyclists with refreshing shade - even in the hottest of summer days. This tunnel of all tunnel of trees is the most northern route in this

Cyclists pause to enjoy the view of Lake Michigan during an organized ride along M-119, Michigan's Tunnel of Trees.

book, a route that ends at Cross Village before looping back.

The ride, which includes 21 miles on M-119, is a tour for experienced cyclists who want the thrill and fun of many ascents and descents. It will challenge and reward your cycle-worthy legs with naturally beautiful scenery, some of the best this region has to offer. Because this area of Emmet County is so devoid of towns and development, there is far less traffic on M-119 than on US-31, the highway most motorists usually take when travelling to Mackinaw City or the Upper Peninsula. The hills for the most part are manageable because of the momentum from the downhills.

Mention Cross Village to anyone who has been there and they

think of one place - Legs Inn. If you can imagine it, Legs Inn (☎ 231-526-2281) is a place that combines a respect of the Indian culture, a Polish heritage and a love of northwest Michigan. It was built by Stanley Smolak, a Chicagoan, who fell in love with the area and moved to Cross Village in 1921. Smolak quickly made friends with the Ottawa Indians, who inducted him into their tribe as "Chief White Cloud." He built the Legs Inn of driftwood and stone he found along the shoreline with unique results. It's a historical landmark with Polish and American cuisine, including outdoor dining overlooking Lake Michigan. There are even lakeside, housekeeping cottages.

Today, Stanley Smolak's ancestors keep the tradition going. "It's weird, this place is weird," said one visitor to the Legs Inn. She was referring to the interior of the place, filled with pieces of driftwood in the shape of different sculptures. At the Legs Inn, they serve Polish entrees including pierogi (stuffed dumplings), gotabki (stuffed cabbage rolls) and bigos (a hearty stew). Plus you can enjoy imported Polish beers (try Krakus). This ethnic restaurant is a great stopover for cyclists - about halfway through the longer loop - before cycling back to the Harbor Springs area.

Harbor Springs, your starting point, is an affluent tourist town. Harbor Springs impresses visitors with its expensive Victorian cottages and the view from "The Bluff" overlooking the water and the picturesque harbor. The business district of Harbor Springs is where you can find boutiques with the latest beachwear or other trendy, upscale clothing. Naturally, there are numerous restaurants. (Hey! Would we do a bike tour where there wasn't?) For ice cream, try Juilleret's (☎ 231-526-2821), the first soda shop in the area or Kilwin's (☎ 231-526-2802). For pizza, it's Turkey's Pizza (☎ 231-526-6041) or, for more of a dining experience, there is The New York (☎ 231-526-1904) and Stafford's Pier (☎ 231-526-6201). As Harbor Springs is a resort town, casual attire (i.e. biking shorts) is acceptable at almost all restaurants.

Stage One (16.7 miles) From the south end of Harbor Springs on M-119, head right (north) on Hoyt Road. Then turn immediately to your left on Lake Road at a two-way stop sign at *Mile 0.2*. Turn right on State Road, also called County Road 77, at almost *Mile 1*. State Road is a lightly travelled, inland road that heads north and in the beginning has gravel shoulders and some rolling hills and open farmland. At *Mile 2* there are paved shoulders on both sides. The road curves to the left and downhill at *Mile 3.4* followed by more curves and a long uphill stretch at *Mile 9.*

A scenic, densely wooded area and a "Welcome to Readmond Township" sign greets you at *Mile 9.6*, and then it's a downhill to the right. Beginning at *Mile 11.4*, you encounter more hills as the road swings to the left, followed by more hills and more twists and more turns in CR-77 at *Mile 13.* This first stage is a long one - no place to stop for refreshments or a bathroom break - so be prepared!

The road narrows with no shoulders at *Mile 14* and then curves to your left as you enter Cross Village at *Mile 16.7.* Turn right on Lakeshore Drive and you will find yourself at the Legs Inn, a "must-stop" on your cycling itinerary. There's also the Cross Village General Store nearby.

But Legs Inn is definitely the attraction here. Outside the inn is bizarre at best; a building of boulders and wood, topped off by inverted stone legs (thus its name) and surrounded by a tipi, totem poles and a figurehead of an Indian chief. The interior is filled with Smolak's polished sculpture - more driftwood than any decent fire marshal would allow if Cross Village had one. The bar itself is one gigantic tree trunk while the doors are made entirely out of knots of wood that took Smolak more than two years to piece together. Don't linger here too long - you're still 21 miles from Harbor Springs.

Stage Two (7.5 miles) Once you've experienced Legs Inn, it is time to begin your cycling adventure on the famous M-119. Head south and M-119 (also called Lake Shore) immediately curves to the right at *Mile 17* and then twists and curves and heads downhill. The shoulders along the road disappear at *Mile 17.4* and within a half mile you're winding uphill. It's okay because shortly you begin pedalling through the road's natural tunnels. This is a hilly stretch along a winding road and where the leafy tunnels end, you're rewarded with a view of Lake Michigan from the edge of a bluff. Spectacular country.

After passing an antique shop at *Mile 18.7* and climbing a long hill at *Mile 19.5* you re-enter Readmond Township. More curves and views of Lake Michigan are passed, along with the junction to Island View Road at 20.7 miles, followed by more tunnels that are spectacular in early October (though at that time of year the vehicle traffic tends to be considerably heavier). There are excellent views of Lake Michigan at *Mile 22.8* and then you enter Good Hart at *Mile 24.2*,

Northwest Michigan

CROSS VILLAGE

16.7 Miles

Lake Shore Dr.

N

SHORT LOOP
Start · 0 Miles
Finish · 18 Miles

GOOD HART

Robinson Rd.

State Rd.

9.6 Miles

119

LAKE MICHIGAN

Stutsmanville Rd.

C77

Middle Rd.

State Rd.

Hoyt Rd.

Lake Rd.

LONG LOOP
Start · 0 Miles
Finish · 38 Miles

HARBOR SPRINGS

Cyclists pause in front of Legs Inn in Cross Village.

where you'll find an antique shop and the Good Hart Store (☎ 231-
-526-7661) which doubles up as a post office. The general store is
open daily and has a deli with a selection of sandwiches as well as
other items, if you didn't eat at the Legs Inn.

Stage Three (14.1 miles) From Good Hart, keep cycling south
on M-119 toward Harbor Springs. More tunnels are encountered as
the road begins to wind downhill at *Mile 25.4*. You're rewarded with
views of Lake Michigan along the way and an antique shop at *Mile
26.4* before challenged by more hills, including an especially steep
one at *Mile 27.4*. You pass the junction to Stutsmanville Road at *Mile
28.6* and another nice view of the lake within a mile. M-119 continues
to twist and curve its way south and you find you are cycling up then
down, hill after hill, in working off your last meal while justifying
another at the end of the tour.

You'll cycle a new housing development, signs that you're
getting close to Harbor Springs, then coast down a long hill at *Mile
32.2* followed (naturally) by an uphill stretch. M-119 curves to the
right at *Mile 32.7*, and then it's up another long hill where on your left
is Birchwood Farm Estate at *Mile 34* followed by the Birchwood Inn
(☎ 231-526-2151, 800-530-9955). The facilities include golf links,

tennis courts, lodging and a restaurant. In the spring and fall, the Birchwood Inn sponsors bike tours along M-119.

You're not far from Harbor Springs now! A loooong downhill stretch is encountered at *Mile 37* and then you pass through a nice residential section in Harbor Springs. The road curves a couple of times to the right and finally you head downhill into Harbor Springs. Turn left at the 3-way stop at *Mile 38*.

If you have a sweet tooth, you will probably notice Kilwin's on the corner for homemade chocolates and ice cream. Antiques, art galleries, upscale clothing, a general store; you'll find it all in Harbor Springs! Turkey's Pizza, the best pizza in town, is on your right. You're back at the starting point on Hoyt Street at *Mile 38.5*. Congratulations- you've just completed the northernmost tour of our West Michigan region.

Shorter Option (18 miles) Park at Good Hart store. Cycle east on Robinson Road to CR-77 (State Road); turn left (north). Stay on CR-77 into Cross Village. From Cross Village, cycle south on M-119 back to starting point in Good Hart.

Bicycle sales, service

Touring Gear, 114 E. Third St., Harbor Springs; ☎ (231) 526-7152.

High Gear, 1187 N. US-31, Petoskey; ☎ (231) 347-6118.

Fitness Source & Cycle, 100 N. Division St., Petoskey; ☎ (231) 347-6877.

Area events and festivals

May: Spring Shoreline Bike Tour, Birchwood Inn, Harbor Springs.

July: Fourth of July Parade & Fireworks, Petoskey & Harbor Springs; Harbor Springs Art Festival; Venetian Festival, Charlevoix.

September: Fall Shoreline Bike Tour, Birchwood Inn.

Travel information

Boyne Country Visitors & Convention Bureau; ☎ (800) 845-2828 or (231) 348-2755, *www.boynecountry.com*.

Petoskey Regional Chamber of Commerce; ☎ (231) 347-4150.

Appendix

Accommodations

Lodging located on or near the routes listed with the corresponding bike tour number. Lodging listed below is just a sampling of the many choices in West Michigan.

Tour 3: Shady Shores Resort, 51256 Garret, Dowagiac, MI 49047; ☎ (616) 424-5251.

Tour 4: Boulevard Inn, 521 Lake Blvd., St. Joseph, MI 49085; ☎ (616) 983-6600.

Tour 5: The Christmere House, 110 Pleasant St., Sturgis, MI 49091; ☎ (616) 651-8303.

Tour 8: Maplewood Hotel, 428 Butler St., Saugatuck, MI 49453; ☎ (616) 857-1771.

Tour 9: Country Inn By Carlson, 12260 James St., Holland, MI 49424; ☎ (616) 396-6677.

Tour 10: Days Inn, 310 Pearl St. NW, Grand Rapids, MI 49504; ☎ (616) 235-7611.

Tour 11: Amerihost Inn, 4677 Harvey Road, Norton Shores, MI 49441; ☎ (616) 798-0220.

Tour 14: Grandma's House Bed & Breakfast, 126 S. Fremont St., Rockford, MI 49341; ☎ (616) 866-4111.

Tour 15: Michillinda Beach Lodge, 5207 Scenic Dr., Whitehall, MI 49461; ☎ (231) 893-1895.

Tour 16: Silver Sands Resort, RR 1 Box 318, Mears, MI 49436; ☎ (231) 873-3769.

Tour 17: Weathervane Inn, 4525 Dowling, Montague, MI 49437;

☎ (877) 893-8931.

Tour 18: Holiday Inn Hotel & Conference Center, 105 Perry St., Big Rapids, MI 49307; ☎ (800) 999-9069.

Tour 19: Lighthouse Motel, 710 W. Ludington Ave., Ludington, MI 49431; ☎ (231) 845-6117.

Tour 20: Best Western Bill Oliver's Resort, M-55 West, P.O. Box 266, Cadillac, MI 49601; ☎ (800) OLIVER-5.

Tour 21: The Beach House, 221 Lake Street, Beulah, MI 49617; ☎ (800) 757-6692.

Tour 23: The Jolli Lodge, M-22, Lake Leelanau, MI 49653; ☎(231) 259-9291.

Tour 25: Heritage Inn, 417 Munson Ave., Traverse City, MI 49686; ☎ (800) 968-0105

Tour 28: Elk River Inn, US-31 at Elk River, Elk Rapids, MI 49629; ☎ (231) 264-5655.

Tour 29: Weathervane Terrace Hotel, 111 Pine River Lane, Charlevoix, MI 49720; ☎ (231) 547-4311.

Tour 30: Birchwood Inn, 7077 Lake Shore Dr., Harbor Springs, MI 49740; ☎ (231)526-2151 or (800) 530-9955.

Additional information

West Michigan Tourist Association, 1253 E. Front St. NW, Grand Rapids, MI 49503; ☎ (616) 456-8557, *www.wmta.org.*

Travel Michigan, P.O. Box 30226, Lansing, MI 48909; ☎ (800) 784-7328.

Michigan Department of Transportation, 425 W. Ottawa St., Lansing, MI 48909; (Send for order blank: individual Michigan county cycling maps available).

League of Michigan Bicyclists, P.O. Box #16201, Lansing, MI 48901; ☎ (888) DRY-BIKE for Shoreline Tours information and a calendar of organized bike tours.

Annual rides in West Michigan

For the current phone numbers to the following tours contact the League of Michigan Bicyclists (see Additional Information above).

May: Kal-Haven Trailblazer, Kalamazoo and South Haven; Harbor Springs Cycling Classic (May and September).

June: The 100 Grand, Grand Rapids; Clean Air Ride, Grand

Rapids; Flag Day Festival Mountain Bike Tour, Three (
Lake Tour, Frankfort; Michigan National 24-Hour Cha
Center; Pedal Across Lower Michigan (PALM), South Haven; Michi-
gan MS 150 Bike Tour, Grand Rapids.

July: Holland Hundred; Ride Around Torch Lake (RAT), Elk
Rapids; Covered Bridge Bike Tour, Lowell; Flowerfest Bicycle Tour,
Kalanazoo; County Ride, Grand Rapids.

August: Shoreline Bicycle Tour, New Buffalo; Heritage Tour,
Kingsley.

September: Leelanau Lakeshore Loop, Suttons Bay; One Day
Ride Across Michigan, Muskegon; Vineyard Classic Bicycle Tour,
Paw Paw; Cereal City Century, Battle Creek; Leelanau Harvest
Tour, Cedar; Apple Cider Century, Three Oaks; Harbor Springs
Cycling Classic; Fall Harvest Tour, Sturgis.

October: Octoberfest, Whitehall; Turning Leaves Century,
Edwardsburg; Great Pumpkin Fest Bike Tour, Zeeland; Colorburst,
Lowell.

West Michigan cycling clubs

Battle Creek Bicycle Club ☎ (616) 660-6266.

Berrien Bicycle Club ☎ (616) 471-3592.

Big Rapids Bicycle Club ☎ (231) 832-2709.

Cherry Capital Cycling Club ☎ (231) 941-BIKE, website: *www.michiweb.com/cycling/index.html.*

Harbor Springs Bicycle Club ☎ (231) 526-7152.

Kalamazoo Bicycle Club ☎ (616) 343-2288, website: *www.angelfire.com/mi/kbc/.*

Muskegon Bicycle Club ☎ (231) 894-8052.

Rapid Wheelman ☎ (616) 752-8123, website: *www.lmb.org/clubs/rapid.htm.*

Three Oaks Spokes Bicycle Club ☎ (616) 756-3311, website: *www.gtm.net/~ronholder/spokes.htm.*

Thornapple Valley Bikers ☎ (616) 948-4149.

Tulip City Two-Wheelers ☎ (616) 335-9591.

Westshore Cycling Club (Grand Haven area) ☎ (616) 842-6626.

Wheel People of St. Joseph County ☎ (616) 651-5088.

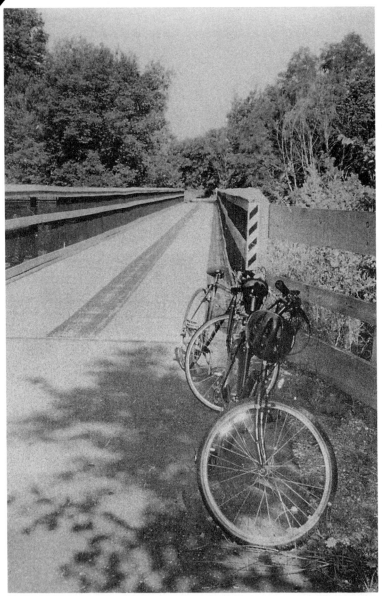

A bridge along the Musketawa Trail, a rail-trail located just west of Grand Rapids.

West Michigan Rail Trails

A system of interconnecting pathways linking Michigan together is the vision of the Rails-to-Trails Conservancy of Michigan.

The movement has taken hold. There are 50 rail trails in Michigan ranging from less than a mile to a 92-mile trail extending from Grand Rpaids to Cadillac. The map on page 216 depicting the existing trails is evidence that the Rails-to-Trails Conservancy's vision may one day be a reality. Slowly - inch by inch, foot by foot, mile by mile - Michigan is preserving its railroad heritage by converting abandoned railroad corridors to recreational trails for cyclists, hikers, horseback riders and in-line skaters.

West Michigan has a substantial number of proposed trails and several of the major existing routes are described in this book. Each of the existing trails has a unique story of how it began, but all became a reality because of collaborating interests and solid working relationships (sometimes unprecedented) between municipalities, trail user groups, the Michigan Department of Natural Resources and the generosity of adjoining landowners.

The Hart-Montague Trail State Park Michigan's first linear state park winds more than 22 miles through the countryside of Oceana and northern Muskegon counties. Bill Field, a private citizen and rail trail advocate, purchased the corridor and gifted it to the state. In its first few months of operation in 1989, an estimated 45,000 recreationists used the trail. The north half of the trail was paved in 1989 and the southern half completed in 1990.

A Michigan National Resources Trust Fund (MNRTF) grant

Rail-Trails: Present & Future

❶ Kal-Haven
❷ Van Buren
❸ Lakelands
❹ Macomb
❺ Paint Creek & Polly Ann
❻ Portland River
❼ Kent
❽ Musketawa
❾ White Pine
❿ Fred Meijer
⓫ Hart-Montague
⓬ Pere Marquette
⓭ Saginaw Valley
⓮ Betsie Valley
⓯ Leelanau & TART
⓰ Cheboygan
⓱ Mackinaw
⓲ Hawks
⓳ Alpena-Hillman

Mackinaw City
Cheboygan
Hawks
Alpena
Gaylord
Suttons Bay
Traverse City
Cadillac
Baldwin
Clare
Reed City
Bay City
Hart
Midland
Montague
Saginaw
Grand Rapids
Portland
Lapeer
Lake Orion
Rochester
South Haven
Kalamazoo
Hamburg
Hartford
Concord
Jackson

assisted the development and the remaining mileage was completed using Department of Natural Resources (DNR) Recreation Improvement Fund (RIF). The trail is managed by the DNR Parks Division as a linear state park. Individual and family permits are required which helps defray operational costs.

Kal-Haven Trail State Park After years of negotiation, the DNR purchased this 34-mile corridor that traverses woods and countryside, using MNRTF funds. The surfacing of the trail (crushed screen limestone and crushed screened cinder slag) began in 1990. Individual and family permits are also required on this trail.

Funds for trail improvements come from the DNR and the Michigan Department of Transportation. The Friends of the Kal-Haven Trail provide additional funding and labor for trail improvement and operation.

Kent Trails With DNR grant assistance, this non-motorized 15-mile corridor that runs from near downtown Grand Rapids to Byron Center opened in 1992. It includes six miles of rail corridor, road sections and paths over a new pipeline. Six governmental bodies help maintain the popular trail, recognized statewide for its contribution to recreation.

Musketawa Trail: The Musketawa Rail-Trail is a 26-mile recreational trail linking Marne to Muskegon. Currently 13 miles of the path is paved from Ravenna to Marne, while the trail from Ravenna to Muskegon is compacted and used by mountain bikers. There are 16 trestles on the Musketawa Trial of which two are more than 200 feet. The Friends of the Musketawa Trail assisted in restoring the railings and decking on the trestles over Crockery Creek and Black Creek. The Crockery Creek trestle includes lookout benches.

Pere Marquette: Orginially the Flint and Pere Marquette Railroad, the Pere Marquette Rail-Trail extends from Midland to Baldwin and will be 84 miles long when completed. It currently crosses the White Pine Trail in Reed City, where it is paved for seven miles east to Patterson Road. It is also paved from Midland to Coleman, a 22-mile stretch.

Traverse Area Recreation Trail (T.A.R.T.): This paved trail is currently 8.6 miles long and extends from Acme to west of Traverse City. In between it winds around the south end of both the East and West bays of Grand Traverse Bay. A portion of the trail is still own by the Michigan Department of Transportation and parallels an

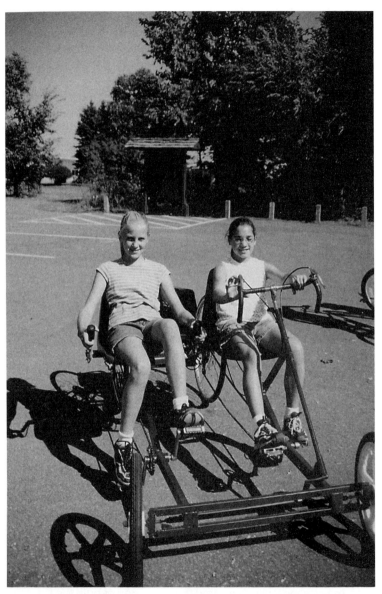

A pair of cyclists prepare to ride their unusual tandem on the Musketawa Rail-Trail west of Grand Rapids.

existing railroad line. Financial support for the trail came from local charities, Grand Traverse County and Friends of TART. In 1998 the Traverse Area Recreation and Transportation Trails, Inc. as a nonprofit organization to manage TART and several other area trails including VASA and the Leelanau Trail.

Leelanau Trail: The Leelanau Trail is a 15-mile rail-trail from Traverse City to Suttons Bay. Currently five miles of the trail are paved just west of Traverse City and future plans call for additional paving and connecting it to the west end of the T.A.R.T. The Leelanau Trail Association was formed to help raise funds to purchase the corridor for the trail. The association not only purchased the railbed but also two cabooses that will eventually serve as trailheads. Presently a paved shoulder along M-22 connects the T.A.R.T. to the Leelanau Trail, creating a 25-mile route from Suttons Bay to Acme.

White Pine Trail State Park The White Pine Trail, the longest linear state park in Michigan, stretches 92 miles from Comstock Park to Cadillac. The trail surface is natural ballast and gravel with the exception of two paved segments; Big Rapids to Reed City and Belmont to Rockford. Formerly the Penn Central Railroad, the trail is managed by the Parks and Recreation Division of the Michigan Department of Natural Resources. The trail crosses 14 open deck bridges through five counties with the longest being the 319-foot Whites Bridge over the Muskegon River.

For more information Cyclists who wish to get involved in the development and planning of Michigan's Rails-to-Trails program should contact the state chapter of the National Rails-To-Trails Conservancy: Rails-to-Trails Conservancy of Michigan, 913 W. Holmes, Suite 227-D, Lansing, MI 48910; ☎ (517) 393-6022, *www.railtrails.org/MI.*

The Author

Karen Gentry, a resident of Grand Rapids, Mich., is currently an editor and writer for a trade publication. She formerly worked for the West Michigan Tourist Association, where she was the project coordinator for the first Lake Michigan Circle Tour Guide. She was also the editor of Trails-a-Way, a regional camping publication, a reporter for a chain of West Michigan newspapers and a high school English and journalism teacher.

Gentry is a journalism graduate of Central Michigan University and a graduate of Lake Michigan Catholic High School in St. Joseph, Mich. Besides cycling, she enjoys other outdoor pursuits such as running and cross country skiing.

Gentry is also the author of *Cycling Michigan: 30 of the Best Bike Routes in East Michigan* and co-author of *Mountain Biking Michigan: The Best Trails in the Upper Peninsula*.

PEGG LEGG
PUBLICATIONS